PLANNING

~ A ~

WEDDING

~ WITH ~

DIVORCED PARENTS

PLANNING
~ A ~
WEDDING
~ WITH ~
DIVORCED PARENTS

Cindy Moore and Tricia Windom

with Martha Giddens Nesbit

CROWN PUBLISHERS, INC.
NEW YORK

Published by Crown Publishers, Inc.,
201 East 50th Street, New York, New York 10022.
Member of the Crown Publishing Group.

CROWN is a trademark of Crown Publishers, Inc.

Manufactured in the United States of America

Library of Congress Cataloging-in-Publication Data

Moore, Cindy.
    Planning a wedding with divorced parents / Cindy Moore and Tricia
    Windom. — 1st ed.
    Includes index.
    1. Weddings—United States—Planning. 2. Adult children of
divorced parents—United States. I. Windom, Tricia. II. Title.
HQ745.M66 1992
395'.22—dc20   91-39795
                                                          CIP

ISBN 0-517-58451-4

Designed by Nancy Kenmore

10 9 8 7 6 5 4 3 2 1

First Edition

To our husbands,
Richard Moore and Herb Windom,
for their love
and support

To our children,
Tracy, Will, Beth, and Kevin,
for the joy and happiness
they have given us

Contents

〜

Contents

Introduction

Where will I seat my stepmother? Who will pay for my wedding gown? What is the appropriate wording for my invitation? How do I write the engagement announcement? For the bride with divorced parents these are only a few of the dozens of confusing questions to be answered. Wedding details are complicated enough, but when divorce is involved, a whole new set of rules is needed. This book is a reference source that every bride and groom with divorced parents, every divorced parent, and every member of their families will want to read and reread during the important months before the wedding. (It can also serve as a resource for wedding directors, photographers, caterers, and others involved with helping couples from divorced families plan their weddings more successfully.)

We realized through our own experiences the need for *Planning a Wedding with Divorced Parents*. When Cindy (who is divorced and remarried) began planning her daughter Tracy's wedding, she found there was precious little information pertaining to weddings where the parents of the wedding couple are divorced, and what information there was was in bits and pieces. She and Tracy bought eight different books with relevant information scattered throughout. And in many cases, there were no answers or suggestions for their particular situation.

Likewise, wedding consultant Tricia was running from one etiquette book to another in search of solutions to sticky problems facing couples with divorced parents. After four years of directing weddings, she found families hungry for advice to guide them through a wedding when relationships between parents were less than ideal.

We found ourselves discussing weddings with divorce situations more and more and, finally, were inspired to write this book, combining views from the mother of the bride as well as the wedding consultant. We hope that this book will spare brides and their families the frustrating research and substantial book-purchasing expense that we suffered. Most important, *Planning a Wedding with Divorced Parents* answers many questions not dealt with in wedding books currently available.

It would be impossible for us to give examples for all the complications that can arise when dealing with divorces and stepfamilies. It is rather our intention to provide examples for the most common situations, in the hope that the wedding couple will be able to use these examples as guidelines in making their own wedding plans. A divorce in the family need not mean that planning the wedding becomes a succession of awkward and hurtful encounters. With careful consideration of everyone's feelings and some good advice, planning your wedding can be the exciting—even joyful—process you always dreamed it would be.

Timetable
and
Checklist

I t is really happening . . . you are getting married! Right away, you want to set a timetable for when you want to accomplish each and every detail. And you'll want a complete checklist to guide you in planning the perfect wedding.

Before you begin working on these essential elements, know in advance that there are certain items on the lists that may indeed be affected if your parents, or your fiancé's parents, are divorced. You need to allow extra time to work out difficult arrangements, and to permit the back-and-forth discussions that are typical when parents are divorced and no longer in constant communication.

The following timetables and checklists are designed to alert you to potential problems so you can avoid them before they happen or, at least, be prepared to handle them if they occur anyway.

A formal wedding can take months to plan. The following list is a six-month schedule. If, however, you live in a metropolitan area, you may need to allow even more time, and should adjust the schedule accordingly. Likewise, the timetable and checklist can be adjusted to fit a much smaller, much simpler wedding as well.

BRIDE'S TIMETABLE AND CHECKLIST

Six to Twelve Months before the Wedding

_____ Obtain a wedding handbook to help plan your wedding.

_____ Consider engaging the services of a wedding director or consultant. (If your parents are divorced, this person can give you valuable help and guidance. Be sure she has experience with weddings involving divorced parents.)

_____ Select a wedding date and time.

_____ Discuss engagement and/or announcement party with your parents. (See Chapter 3, "The Engagement Party.")

_____ Discuss wedding budget with your parents. (Before you begin discussions, refer to Chapter 2, "The Wedding Budget," so that you will be knowledgeable about the traditional way expenses are handled. Who pays for the wedding and related expenses is one of the most important decisions related to the wedding, and affects many of the other aspects, from size to invitations.)

_____ Decide on the type of wedding and reception you want. Formal or informal? Large or small? (See Chapter 7, "The Wedding Ceremony," and Chapter 9, "The Reception.")

_____ Reserve the location for the ceremony and the reception.

_____ Determine who will officiate at the ceremony.

_____ Decide on your color scheme.

_____ Decide on your wedding style or theme.

_____ Determine the size of your guest list. (Be sure to consult both of your parents about their lists, as well as the groom and his parents.)

_____ Prepare names and addresses for guest lists.

_____ Select wedding attendants.

_____ Plan reception. Make all the reservations with caterer if necessary.

_____ Choose your wedding cake caterer.

_____ Choose musicians for wedding ceremony and reception.

_____ Select a photographer and a video cameraperson.

_____ Select a florist.

_____ Choose your wedding dress, veil, and accessories.

_____ Select your bridesmaids' dresses.

_____ Announce your engagement in the newspaper. (Consult Chapter 4, "The Newspaper Announcement," for correct wording of your announcement.)

_____ Discuss honeymoon plans with your fiancé.

_____ If you will be traveling abroad, update your passport and arrange for visas. Check on your inoculations.

_____ Decide where you will live after the wedding.

Four Months before the Wedding

_____ Order invitations or announcements. (Consult Chapter 5, "Invitations," for correct wording.)

_____ Order personal stationery for thank-you notes.

_____ Visit your clergy or other officiant with your fiancé.

_____ Make final arrangements for ceremony. Deposits should be made and contracts signed.

_____ Help select groom's and men's wedding attire.

_____ Help mothers and stepmothers coordinate and select their dresses.

_____ Check marriage license requirements in your state.

_____ Make appointment for physical exam.

_____ Begin shopping for wedding rings.

_____ Begin shopping for wedding trousseau.

_____ Select your china, crystal, and silver patterns. Register at a bridal registry in the towns of all families.

_____ Plan rehearsal dinner or party with groom and his parents. (Consult Chapter 6, "The Rehearsal Dinner or Party," if groom's parents are divorced.)

Two Months before the Wedding

_____ Address invitations or announcements. Invitations should be mailed four to six weeks before the wedding. (Consult chapter 5.)

_____ Finalize reception plans:

_____ Location

_____ Caterer

_____ Photographer and video cameraperson

_____ Florist

_____ Cake caterer

_____ Musicians

_____ Finalize ceremony details with officiant, custodian, and musicians.

_____ Arrange accommodations for out-of-town attendants or guests.

_____ Make rehearsal arrangements. (It is important that all parents and stepparents attend the rehearsal if they are to be formally seated. Consult chapter 6.)

_____ Notify bridesmaids about their fittings and accessories.

_____ Select bridesmaids' and groomsmen's gifts.

_____ Set date for bridesmaids' luncheon and bachelor party.

_____ Select groom's gift, if gifts are being exchanged.

_____ Final fitting for wedding dress.

_____ Finalize honeymoon plans.

One Month before the Wedding

_____ Obtain marriage license.

_____ Have formal bridal portrait taken.

_____ Send wedding announcement and picture to newspapers. (Consult chapter 4.)

_____ If your wedding gifts will be displayed, set up tables now.

_____ Record all gifts as they arrive and write thank-you notes immediately.

_____ Check on floater insurance policy to cover wedding gifts.

_____ Make transportation arrangements for wedding day.

_____ Complete trousseau purchases and going-away outfit.

_____ Make sure you have all accessories for the wedding and reception: cake knife (two if there is going to be a groom's cake), toasting goblets, ring pillow, garter, candles, etc.

_____ Select person to handle guest book, and determine its location at reception.

_____ Arrange parking attendant for wedding ceremony and/or reception.

_____ Prepare reception agenda.

Two Weeks before the Wedding

_____ Confirm accommodation arrangements for out-of-town guests.

_____ Design maps and make schedule of events for wedding party, family, and out-of-town guests.

_____ Acquire necessary forms for name changes (if you plan to take your husband's last name) on driver's license, social security card, insurance and medical plans, and bank accounts.

_____ Take a change-of-address card to the post office.

_____ Complete addressing announcements that will be mailed on your wedding day.

_____ Make appointment with hairdresser and manicurist for your wedding day.

_____ Meet with photographer to plan pictures. (Consult Chapter 8, "Photography and Video.")

One Week before the Wedding

_____ Give a final estimate of number of reception guests to caterer.

_____ Go over final details:

  _____ Ceremony location

  _____ Reception location

  _____ Caterer

  _____ Photographer and video cameraperson

  _____ Florist

  _____ Cake caterer

  _____ Musicians

_____ Plan seating arrangements. (See chapters 6, 7, and 9.)

_____ Discuss final plans with wedding director or coordinator.

_____ Keep up with thank-you notes.

_____ Begin to pack your suitcase for your honeymoon.

_____ Finalize ceremony details with officiant, organist, soloist, and sexton.

_____ Make sure all wedding attendants have wedding attire.

_____ Present bridesmaids' and flowergirl's gifts at the bridesmaids' luncheon.

_____ Remind groom to present groomsmen's and ring bearer's gifts at the rehearsal dinner or party.

_____ Remind wedding attendants of ceremony and reception time schedule.

_____ Go over special seating or pew cards with usher and/or wedding director. (See chapter 7.)

On Your Wedding Day

_____ Be sure to eat something light and energy-packed, such as pasta.

_____ Have hair and nails done.

_____ If pictures are being taken before the ceremony, be sure all of the wedding party and family members are ready in plenty of time. Check with your photographer. (See chapter 8 concerning family pictures.)

_____ Take going-away clothes to reception location.

_____ Give the honor attendant the groom's ring.

_____ Be sure honeymoon clothes are packed.

_____ Enjoy your special day!

GROOM'S TIMETABLE AND CHECKLIST

Six to Twelve Months before the Wedding

_____ Purchase the bride's engagement ring.

_____ Discuss with fiancée the date and time of wedding.

_____ If you'll be sharing wedding expenses, discuss this with your fiancée and all parents involved. (Refer to Chapter 2, "The Wedding Budget.")

_____ Discuss rehearsal dinner or party plans with your parents. (See Chapter 6, "The Rehearsal Dinner or Party.")

_____ Start making out your guest list. (If your parents are divorced, be sure to consult both parents for their lists.)

_____ Select wedding attendants.

_____ Start making honeymoon plans.

_____ If you will be traveling abroad, update your passport, arrange for visas, and check on your inoculations.

_____ Decide where you will live after the wedding.

Four Months before the Wedding

_____ Select men's wedding attire.

_____ Shop with fiancée for wedding rings.

_____ Complete your guest list.

_____ Check marriage license requirements in your state.

_____ Visit your clergy or other officiant with your fiancée.

_____ Finalize all honeymoon plans, and send in deposits if required.

_____ Plan rehearsal dinner or party with bride and your parents. (Consult chapter 6.)

Two Months before the Wedding

_____ Have groomsmen reserve their wedding attire.

_____ Assist parents with plans for rehearsal dinner or party. (Refer to chapter 6 if your parents are divorced.)

_____ Meet with clergy or officiant to finalize ceremony details.

_____ Discuss with the florist the flowers that are traditionally your financial responsibility. (See chapter 2.)

_____ Arrange accommodations for out-of-town attendants.

_____ Select bride's gift, if gifts are being exchanged.

_____ Set date for bachelor party.

One Month before the Wedding

_____ Obtain marriage license.

_____ Check that all attendants have ordered their wedding attire and been fitted.

_____ Purchase gifts for groomsmen.

_____ Pick up wedding rings.

Two Weeks before the Wedding

_____ Arrange wedding day transportation.

_____ Confirm accommodations for groomsmen.

_____ If moving, notify post office of change of address. Arrange to have utilities turned on in new home.

_____ Have your hair cut.

One Week before the Wedding

_____ Discuss final details with fiancée, and offer to assist.

_____ Pick up wedding attire.

_____ Make sure attendants get their wedding attire.

_____ Begin to pack clothes for honeymoon.

_____ Confirm honeymoon plans.

_____ Make sure attendants know rehearsal time schedule.

_____ Go over special seating or pew cards with ushers and/or wedding director. (See Chapter 7, "The Wedding Ceremony.")

_____ Go over rehearsal dinner or party plans with parents, including seating arrangements. (See chapter 6.)

_____ Present gifts to your attendants at the rehearsal dinner or party.

On Your Wedding Day

_____ Be sure to eat something.

_____ Put clergy or officiant's fee in a sealed envelope and give it to the best man to present after the ceremony.

_____ Make sure luggage is in the car or at the hotel where you will stay tonight.

_____ Give the best man the bride's wedding band.

_____ Take the marriage license to the ceremony.

_____ If pictures are being taken before the ceremony, be sure you, your family, and your attendants are ready in plenty of time. (See Chapter 8, "Photography and Video.")

_____ Enjoy your special day!

2

The
Wedding
Budget

Jennifer knew she had found her wedding dress the minute she saw it. It had a high neck, long, tight sleeves, and a fitted bodice to show off her trim figure.

"Oh, darling, it's perfect!" said her mother, catching her breath when she saw Jennifer in the dress for the first time.

Jennifer had shopped early and, with that major detail out of the way, put the matter of the dress out of her mind. Soon, she was caught up in a thousand other details: planning the menu for the reception, listening to tapes to select just the right music for the wedding, shopping for bridesmaids' gifts, and addressing invitations. Orchestrating a wedding, she thought at one point, was like having a full-time job.

When it came time to discuss finances, Jennifer believed she had covered her bases. Her mother, Amanda, and her father, Steve, had been divorced for several years. They would not agree to sit down together to work out all the financial details, but they were polite and understanding in discussing the finances with Jennifer. Jennifer had no formal budget, but had a pretty good idea about how much things were going to cost. Her parents were very clear about how much they were willing to spend. Jennifer was willing to make some compromises, but still, the wedding would be lovely.

The wedding day was perfect. The dress, Jennifer thought later when she had time to reflect, had been the right choice. She had known that the minute she saw the look in Gordon's eyes when he saw her coming down the aisle.

After the honeymoon, Jennifer and Gordon began to set up their new home. A few bills trickled in, and because they were small, Jennifer and Gordon went ahead and paid them themselves. No need to trouble her parents, and besides, most of the bills were for little extras Jennifer had forgotten all about and certainly hadn't mentioned in the conversations she had had with her parents.

One afternoon after work, Jennifer was going through the mail and came upon a letter that made her heart pound. She ripped open the Bridal Boutique envelope, hands shaking. The bill read: "Wedding Dress: $2,000."

Difficult as it was to believe, she had forgotten all about it! She had selected it so long ago! Her mother had assumed, because Jennifer had never discussed it, that her father was paying for it. Her father never thought about anything unless Jennifer brought it to his attention.

After Jennifer spoke with both parents, they agreed to each pay for a third of the dress, and that Jennifer and Gordon should take responsibility for a third as well. Jennifer and Gordon couldn't afford it, and would have to pay a small amount each month. But it wasn't right to leave her parents to pay such a large sum. Had she remembered the expense of the dress, Jennifer could easily have cut back somewhere else in her wedding plans. Why, oh why, hadn't she made out a formal checklist? Then, surely, she would never have made such an oversight!

Expenses: Who Pays for What?

The bride's family is traditionally responsible for most of the wedding ceremony costs, as well as for the costs of the reception. The groom's family, on the other hand, is generally responsible for the rehearsal dinner or party costs. However, there are no set rules about who pays for what, and each wedding may vary as special circumstances arise.

When the bride's parents are divorced, budget decisions should be made with the feelings of both parents in mind, no matter who pays the bills. Communication between the bride and both of her parents is absolutely essential from the beginning. A wedding coordinator or someone knowledgeable in this area could be of great help in presenting ideas to the bride, her mother, and her father about the many ways expenses can be handled.

Start with the expenses checklist from this chapter. Provide a copy for your mother and your father. If it is not possible for the three of you to sit down together to talk, the bride may have to meet with each parent individually and try to divide the expenses fairly. She will probably want to allow some time for changes, compromises, and discussions as her parents think about their financial decisions.

Dividing the expenses will give you a starting point, and will lead off early to an open discussion about the many costs involved. Whatever is decided, everyone should know about, and agree upon, who is paying for what.

There may be circumstances in which one of the bride's parents is financially able to contribute to the wedding costs but refuses to do so. In that case, the bride should not feel obligated to include that parent in any of the planning. She may choose to include the parent as an honored guest, not for the parent's sake, but for her own happiness and for the future of their relationship.

If the groom's parents are divorced, his financial responsibilities should be discussed with his parents from the beginning, also. Communication is essential! The groom's expense checklist is included in this chapter. The groom should provide a copy for his mother and his father. Decisions should be made early about who will be paying for what. There may be circumstances when one of the groom's parents refuses to contribute to the costs of the rehearsal dinner or party even though financially able to do so. If this happens, the groom should not feel obligated to include that parent in any of the planning. He may choose to include the parent as an honored guest at the rehearsal dinner or party and at the wedding.

Both the bride and groom should realize from the start that unless they have an unlimited budget, they will probably have to compromise on their wedding plans. That doesn't mean that you have to sacrifice in any way! By planning ahead and thinking creatively, you can still have many of the special extras that you feel are important. Your objective is to have a happy day that you will always remember. How much you spend is not the issue.

CHARTS MAKE IT EASIER

To enable you and your parents to divide the financial responsibilities and keep accurate records during your planning, use the expense checklists and worksheets included in this chapter. They will help you decide who is paying for what, and keep track of what you ordered, the total price, the deposit given, and the balance due.

EXPENSES FOR BRIDE AND/OR HER FAMILY

Bride / Mother / Father /

_____ _____ _____ Services of a bridal consultant or director

_____ _____ _____ Engagement party (optional)

_____ _____ _____ Ceremony location: rental, custodial fee, police fee, and/or parking attendant fee

_____ _____ _____ Ceremony music: soloists, organist, pianist, instrumentalists, etc.

_____ _____ _____ Ceremony rentals: candles, aisle cloth, etc.

_____ _____ _____ Ceremony flowers: decorations; bride's bouquet (unless groom is providing); groom's boutonniere; bridesmaids' bouquets and hairpieces; flowergirl's bouquet or basket and hairpiece; ring bearer's pillow; corsage for mothers, stepmothers, grandmothers, and others (unless groom is providing); boutonnieres for ushers and fathers, stepfathers, grandfathers, and others (unless groom is providing)

――	――	――	Bride's wedding attire and accessories
――	――	――	Wedding invitations, announcements, personal stationery, calligrapher, and mailing costs
――	――	――	Other related expenses of the ceremony
――	――	――	Photography and video
――	――	――	Transportation of bridal party and bride and groom to the ceremony and reception
――	――	――	Fees for police and/or parking attendants at reception
――	――	――	Rental fee for the reception location
――	――	――	Food and beverages for the reception
――	――	――	Entertainment for the reception
――	――	――	Rental items for the reception
――	――	――	Floral decorations for the reception
――	――	――	Wedding cake
――	――	――	Bride's trousseau
――	――	――	Groom's ring
――	――	――	Wedding gift for groom, if gifts are being exchanged
――	――	――	Bridesmaids' gifts
――	――	――	Bridesmaids' luncheon (if you are hosting)
――	――	――	Accommodations for out-of-town bridesmaids
――	――	――	Moving expenses

EXPENSES FOR GROOM AND/OR HIS FAMILY

Groom / *Mother* / *Father*

Groom	Mother	Father	
____	____	____	Bride's engagement and wedding rings
____	____	____	Rehearsal dinner or party
____	____	____	Personal wedding attire
____	____	____	Groomsmen's gifts
____	____	____	Accommodations for groomsmen
____	____	____	Gloves, ties, and ascots for groomsmen
____	____	____	Bachelor party (if you are hosting)
____	____	____	Ceremony officiant's fee or donation
____	____	____	Marriage license and blood test fees
____	____	____	Bride's flowers (bouquet and going-away corsage)
____	____	____	Wedding gift for bride, if gifts are being exchanged
____	____	____	Corsages for mothers, stepmothers, and grandmothers
____	____	____	Boutonnieres for ushers, fathers, stepfathers, and grandfathers
____	____	____	Transportation after reception
____	____	____	Honeymoon expenses
____	____	____	Moving expenses
____	____	____	Any general expenses to which you may wish to contribute

BRIDE'S WEDDING EXPENSE RECORD

Engagement Party	Estimate	Actual Cost	Deposit	Amount Due
Invitations				
Food				
Beverages				
Entertainment				
Floral decorations				
Rental items				

Ceremony Costs	Estimate	Actual Cost	Deposit	Amount Due
Bridal consultant or director				
Location				
Rental				
Custodial fee				
Police fee and/or parking attendant fee				
Music				
Soloists				
Organist				
Pianist				
Instrumentalists				
Other				
Rentals				

Ceremony Costs	Estimate	Actual Cost	Deposit	Amount Due
Candles				
Aisle cloth				
Other				

Flowers	Estimate	Actual Cost	Deposit	Amount Due
Decorations				
Bride's bouquet (unless groom is providing)				
Groom's boutonniere				
Bridesmaids' bouquets and hairpieces				
Flowergirl's bouquet or basket and hairpiece				
Ring bearer's pillow				
Corsages (unless groom is providing)				
Mothers'				
Stepmothers'				
Grandmothers'				
Other				
Boutonnieres (unless groom is providing)				
Ushers'				
Fathers'				
Stepfathers'				

Flowers	Estimate	Actual Cost	Deposit	Amount Due
Grandfathers'				
Other				

Other Related Expenses	Estimate	Actual Cost	Deposit	Amount Due
Bride's wedding attire				
Wedding dress				
Wedding veil				
Accessories				
Invitations and/or announcements				
Engraving or printing				
Personal stationery				
Calligrapher				
Mailing costs				
Photography and video				
Bride and groom's wedding album				
Bride's mother's photographs				
Bride's father's photographs				
Bride and groom's videotape				
Bride's mother's videotape				

Other Related Expenses	Estimate	Actual Cost	Deposit	Amount Due
Bride's father's videotape				
Transportation				
Bridal party to ceremony				
Bride and groom from ceremony to reception				
Bridal party from ceremony to reception				
Bride and groom from reception (unless groom is providing)				
Bride's trousseau				
Bride's clothes				
Bride's lingerie				
Bride's accessories				
Groom's ring				
Groom's wedding gift				
Bridesmaids' gifts				
Bridesmaids' luncheon				
Accommodations for out-of-town brides-maids				
Moving expenses				
Other				

Reception Costs	Estimate	Actual Cost	Deposit	Amount Due
Location rental				
Caterer or food				
Beverages				
Entertainment				
Rental items				
Floral decorations				
Table arrangements				
Throw-away bouquet				
Corsages for servers				
Wedding cake				
Groom's cake				
Police fee and/or parking attendant fee				

Groom's Wedding Expense Record

Traditional Expenses	Estimate	Actual Cost	Deposit	Amount Due
Bride's rings				
Engagement				
Wedding				
Groom's wedding attire				
Groomsmen's gifts				
Accommodations for out-of-town grooms-men				

GROOM'S WEDDING EXPENSE RECORD

Traditional Expenses	Estimate	Actual Cost	Deposit	Amount Due
Bachelor party				
Gloves, ties, and ascots for groomsmen				
Ceremony officiant's fee				
Marriage license and blood test				
Bride's wedding gift				
Transportation after reception				
Honeymoon expenses				
Moving expenses				
Other				

Rehearsal Dinner or Party Costs	Estimate	Actual Cost	Deposit	Amount Due
Invitations				
Location rental				
Caterer or food				
Beverages				
Entertainment				
Rental items				
Floral decorations				
Police fee and/or parking attendant fee				

The Wedding Budget

Flowers	Estimate	Actual Cost	Deposit	Amount Due
Bride's bouquet				
Corsages				
Bride's going-away				
Mothers'				
Stepmothers'				
Grandmothers'				
Other				
Boutonnieres				
Ushers'				
Fathers'				
Stepfathers'				
Grandfathers'				
Other				

3

The Engagement Party

When Jennifer and Gordon announced their engagement to Jennifer's mother, Amanda, she instantly told them she wanted to give them a big engagement party, a special evening to share their news with family and close friends. Jennifer said that she particularly wanted to invite her father and his new wife, and Amanda went along with the request for the sake of her daughter.

The invitations went out a month before the party, and the responses quickly began to arrive. A week before the party, Amanda still hadn't heard from Jennifer's father and stepmother. She asked her daughter about it. "He said he didn't think he was coming," Jennifer said in the offhanded tone her mother recognized as the one she used when she was hurt, but didn't want her mother to know it.

Jennifer didn't know how to take her father's reaction to the party. She knew it would be awkward for him to attend with Judy, his new wife, but she felt that he could put aside his feelings for one night—for her. She was a little embarrassed, too, that he hadn't formally responded to her mother's invitation.

The night of the party came. There had still been no word from her father and her stepmother about whether or not they would attend. Jennifer watched her mother for any signs of distress. Amanda was so busy, she didn't seem to be thinking about her ex-husband at all. She was, as always, the perfect hostess, poised and gracious and interested in her guests. But Jennifer kept glancing at the door. She tried not to, but she couldn't help herself. She realized how much it would have meant to have her father there.

After it was over, Jennifer, Gordon, and Amanda collapsed on the couch. "I loved the party, Mother, but I missed Daddy," Jennifer admitted. "I wish that I had pinned him down about whether or not he was coming. I wish I had talked with Judy and told her how important it was for them to be here. I suppose I was too casual about the whole thing. It wasn't fair to you, Mother, not to know. And it wasn't fair to me either. It's taught me that from here on out, I'm going to be specific about my feelings. He's going to know that I want everyone involved in this wedding, and somehow, I'm going to pull it off."

Planning the Engagement Party

The engagement party, if the bride and groom choose to have one, will be their first prewedding party. Chances are, when there is a divorce, this is the party that brings into focus some of the problems that will persist throughout the wedding activities. It may be that in planning this party, the bride and her mother realize they need a wedding consultant or planner who can act as a mediator and guide for all of the wedding plans.

If the engagement is going to be announced in the newspaper (see Chapter 4, "The Newspaper Announcement"), the engagement party should ideally take place the night before the announcement appears. However, since most newspapers will rarely guarantee a publication date, this is almost impossible to count on. Therefore, it is quite acceptable to have the party before the newspaper announcement, or shortly thereafter. The newspaper announcement is usually made two or three months before the wedding, although it can appear up to a year before the wedding date or as close as a week before. Accordingly, the engagement party may take place anywhere from one year to one week before the wedding. Ideally, it should be held approximately three months before the wedding.

The party may be as formal or informal as the bride and the host choose, and in keeping with the customs of the town in which they live. The party is usually for family and close friends, but there may be times when they choose to have a large open house or reception.

Engagement parties are usually given by the bride's parents or one of her relatives. However, anyone can give the party, and if the bride's parents are divorced, it is often better for a family friend or the groom's family to give the party. This eliminates choosing which of the bride's parents will act as host.

No matter who is hosting the party, the bride and her mother should make a guest list, which should include their family and friends, the wedding party, and the groom's parents. The bride should ask the groom and his parents for a list, which includes their family and friends. Whether or not to invite stepfamilies is something the bride and groom should consider carefully, but generally, unless the stepfamilies (stepbrothers, stepsisters, and/or stepgrandparents) are close to the bride or groom, they should not be included.

If the bride's mother or her mother and stepfather are hosting the party, the bride should ask her father for his list also, if he is planning to attend. He certainly should be invited to the party, along with his wife, if he has remarried. If she is a "controversial" stepparent, the bride's father may choose to attend the party alone, or not at all, in which case he and his wife may prefer to entertain the couple themselves at a later date. The same would apply for the bride's mother, should the bride's father host the party.

If neither parent has remarried and they are friendly, they may choose to host the engagement party together. Or, if the bride's parents are divorced and one or both are remarried, her mother and father may choose to host the engagement party together, with the stepparents attending as guests.

If the bride's father has remarried and the bride is close to both her mother and her stepmother, the three of them, if they are friendly, may choose to host the party together. The same applies if the bride's mother has remarried and the bride is close to her father and her stepfather.

If both parents are remarried, both couples, if friendly, may choose to host the engagement party together. Remember that whoever hosts the party—parents, stepparents, or a combination of the two—has his or her name included on the invitation.

Sometimes, the bride may find that relations are so strained between her parents that she and the groom may choose to host the party themselves, or let a friend or relative host it for them. Remember, this party is optional, and there may be circumstances when the bride decides that it is simpler and less stressful *not* to have an engagement party.

Announcing the Engagement at the Party

The invitation may have let the guests know that the engagement is "official." If, however, the host and/or hostess decided to try a surprise announcement, they may tell guests as they arrive, or they may choose a special toast at the appropriate time. If the host and/or hostess choose to tell the guests as they arrive, the engaged couple and the host and/or hostess may want to form a receiving line near the door to greet their guests with their news.

Toasting

Toasting at an engagement party is not mandatory. If, however, a toast is to be made, traditionally the father of the bride, the stepfather, the bride's grandfather, an uncle, or a special male friend should make the first toast. However, the bride's mother may choose to make the first toast, especially if she is hosting the party.

If the party is a dinner, the host or hostess will see that all glasses are filled, and then will raise his or her glass and say something like "I propose a toast to Jennifer and Gordon and their happiness." The groom may then want to make a short toast, perhaps thanking family and friends for their good wishes.

Wording the Invitation

Wording the invitation will not be difficult if relatives or family friends are hosting the party. If, however, the bride's parents are divorced and one or both choose to host the party, then consideration must be given to the wording of the invitation.

Wording the invitation also depends on the formality of the party and whether the engagement announcement is planned to be a surprise during the party. Keeping a secret is usually not successful, however, and more often the reason for the party is made clear on the invitation. It is acceptable to issue the invitation by an informal handwritten note or by telephone.

Everyone's engagement party situation is different. The invitation examples in this chapter are designed to address some of the more common ones.

Engagement Party Invitation Examples

For each of the following situations, we provide a formal and an informal invitation example. Look through the list to select the situation that best applies to your particular case, then see the sample invitations for wording ideas.

1. *Neither of bride's parents remarried; hosting party together*

2. *Bride's mother not remarried; hosting party alone*

3. *Bride's father not remarried; hosting party alone*

4. *Bride's mother and/or father remarried; only bride's parents hosting party with stepparents attending as guests*

5. *Only bride's father remarried; father, stepmother, and bride's mother hosting party*

6. *Only bride's mother remarried; mother, stepfather, and bride's father hosting party*

7. *Bride's father and stepmother hosting party*

8. *Bride's mother and stepfather hosting party*

9. *Both bride's parents remarried and bride close to all; all four hosting party*

10. *Bride and groom hosting their own party*

1. Neither of bride's parents remarried; hosting party together

Mrs. Amanda Clark Jones

and

Mr. Steven Riley Jones

cordially invite you to

The Engagement Party

honoring

Jennifer Lee Jones

and

Gordon Floyd Bland

Saturday, the fifth of May

eight o'clock in the evening

2561 Cherokee Road

Please Respond	*Mrs. Amanda Jones*
by April 15th	*34 Broward Court*
	Atlanta, Georgia 30305

Engagement Party
honoring
Jennifer and Gordon
Saturday, May 5th
7:30 p.m.
The Plantation Club

Amanda Jones   Steven Jones

Rsvp
Amanda Jones
355-6724

Responses are usually made to the bride's mother, but this is a decision to be made by those hosting the party.

2. Bride's mother not remarried; hosting party alone

Mrs. Amanda Clark Jones
invites you for
Cocktails
honoring
Jennifer Jones and Gordon Bland
Saturday, the fifth of May
six until eight o'clock
Forest Heights Country Club

Rsvp
by April 15th

34 Broward Court
Atlanta, Georgia 30305

ENGAGEMENT PARTY

OYSTER ROAST
honoring
JENNIFER AND GORDON
SATURDAY, MAY 5th
7:00 p.m.
34 BROWARD COURT

AMANDA JONES

RSVP
355-6724

3. Bride's father not remarried; hosting party alone

Mr. Steven Riley Jones
cordially invites you to
The Engagement Party
honoring
Jennifer Lee Jones
and
Gordon Floyd Bland
Saturday, the fifth of May
eight o'clock in the evening
2561 Cherokee Road
Atlanta, Georgia

Please Respond
by April 15th

2561 Cherokee Road
Atlanta, Georgia 30305

ENGAGEMENT PARTY
HONORING
JENNIFER AND GORDON
SATURDAY, MAY 5th
7:30 p.m.
2561 CHEROKEE ROAD
ATLANTA, GEORGIA

STEVEN JONES

RSVP
233-6435

4. Bride's mother and/or father remarried; only bride's parents hosting party with stepparents attending as guests

Mrs. Glenn Simpson
and
Mr. Steven Jones
invite you to join them
in celebrating the engagement of
Jennifer Jones and Gordon Bland
Saturday, the fifth of May
four until six o'clock
1524 Habersham Way

Please respond to: 1524 Habersham Way
Mrs. Glenn Simpson   Atlanta, Georgia 30305

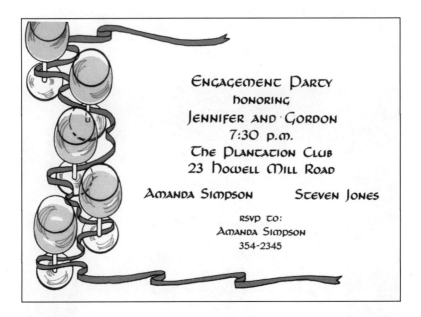

Responses are usually made to the bride's mother, but this is a decision to be made by those hosting the party.

5. *Only bride's father remarried; father, stepmother, and bride's mother hosting party*

Bride's mother's name appears first.

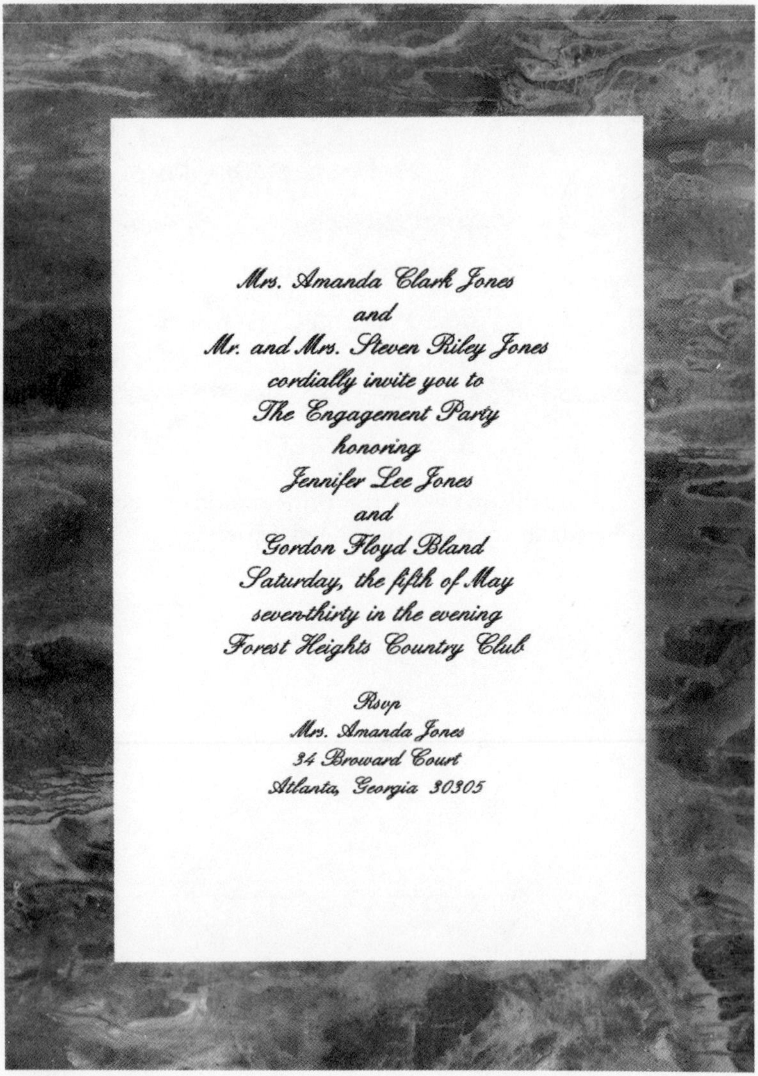

Mrs. Amanda Clark Jones
and
Mr. and Mrs. Steven Riley Jones
cordially invite you to
The Engagement Party
honoring
Jennifer Lee Jones
and
Gordon Floyd Bland
Saturday, the fifth of May
seven-thirty in the evening
Forest Heights Country Club

Rsvp
Mrs. Amanda Jones
34 Broward Court
Atlanta, Georgia 30305

ENGAGEMENT PARTY
HONORING
JENNIFER AND GORDON
SATURDAY, MAY 5th
7:30 P.M.

THE CHEROKEE COUNTRY CLUB

AMANDA JONES *   JANE AND STEVEN JONES

* RSVP
355-6724

Responses are usually made to the bride's mother, but this is a decision to be made by those hosting the party.

6. *Only bride's mother remarried; mother, stepfather, and bride's father hosting party*

Bride's mother's and stepfather's names appear first.

Mr. and Mrs. Glenn Richards Simpson
and
Mr. Steven Riley Jones
cordially invite you to
The Engagement Party
honoring
Jennifer Lee Jones
and
Gordon Floyd Bland
Saturday, the fifth of May
seven thirty in the evening
Forest Heights Country Club

Please respond
by April fifteenth

Mrs. Glenn Richards Simpson
152 Habersham Way
Atlanta, Georgia 30305

ENGAGEMENT PARTY
honoring
JENNIFER
AND
GORDON
SATURDAY, MAY 5th
7:30 p.m.
The Cherokee Country Club

Amanda and Glenn Simpson
Steven Jones

RSVP to:
Amanda Simpson   354-2345

Responses are usually made to the bride's mother, but this is a decision to be made by those hosting the party.

7. Bride's father and stepmother hosting party

Mr. and Mrs. Steven Riley Jones
cordially invite you to a
Cocktail Buffet
honoring
Jennifer Jones and Gordon Bland
Saturday, May fifth
at eight o'clock
The Plantation Club

Please respond to:
2200 Piedmont Road
Atlanta, Georgia 30329

PLEASE JOIN US
FOR THE
ENGAGEMENT PARTY
HONORING
JENNIFER AND GORDON
SATURDAY, MAY 5TH
7:30 P.M.
THE COMMODORE CLUB

JANE AND STEVEN JONES

PLEASE REPLY   233-6435

8. Bride's mother and stepfather hosting party

Mr. and Mrs. Glen Richards Simpson
invite you for
Cocktails
Honoring the Engagement of
Jennifer Jones and Gordon Bland
Saturday, May fifth
six until eight o'clock
Forest Heights Country Club

Rsvp
1524 Habersham Way
Atlanta, Georgia 30305

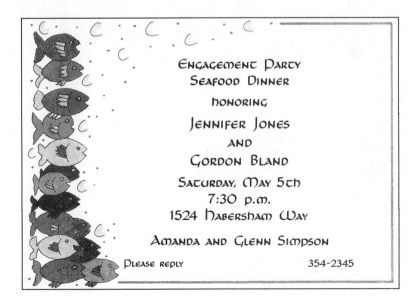

ENGAGEMENT PARTY
SEAFOOD DINNER

HONORING

JENNIFER JONES
AND
GORDON BLAND

SATURDAY, MAY 5TH
7:30 P.M.
1524 HABERSHAM WAY

AMANDA AND GLENN SIMPSON

PLEASE REPLY   354-2345

9. *Both bride's parents remarried and bride close to all; all four hosting party*

Bride's mother's and stepfather's names appear first.

Mr. and Mrs. Glen Richards Simpson
and
Mr. and Mrs. Steven Riley Jones
cordially invite you to
The Engagement Party
honoring
Jennifer and Gordon
Saturday, May 5th   *8:00 p.m.*
1524 Habersham Way

Please reply   *1524 Habersham Way*
Mrs. Glenn Richards Simpson   *Atlanta, Georgia 30305*

Engagement Party
honoring
Jennifer and Gordon

Saturday, May 5th
7:30 p.m.

The Plantation Club

Amanda and Glenn Simpson
Jane and Steven Jones

RSVP
Amanda Simpson
354-2345

Responses are usually made to the bride's mother, but this is a decision to be made by those hosting the party.

10. *Bride and groom hosting their own party*

Cocktail Buffet
to celebrate our engagement
Saturday, May 5th
7:00 p.m.
2564 Wright Way
Jennifer and Gordon
Rsvp   *2368745*

4

The
Newspaper
Announcement

Jennifer's parents divorced when she was a young child. And although neither had remarried, there was much bitterness. Most of the time, Jennifer could handle being caught in the middle of her parents' disagreements, particularly after she was old enough to be on her own in her own apartment. That way, she could talk privately by phone with her mother, and with her father, too. But when her parents were together for family events, Jennifer was an emotional wreck, trying to make sure both were happy, worrying that one would embarrass the other, or that both would embarrass themselves.

The state of her parents' relationship was never more evident than at her brothers' weddings, when her mother openly ridiculed her father in front of family, friends, and even innocent bystanders. For this reason, Jennifer decided on a private wedding, with just her mother and her fiancé's parents invited. It was not what she wanted, but it was what she was prepared to do rather than have her parents feuding on her special day.

When Jennifer began to think about the newspaper engagement announcement, she called her mother for advice on how the wording should be. "I'd prefer that you didn't even mention your father," said her mother in the hurt voice she always used when she discussed her ex-husband. "He's never been much of a father anyway." In exasperation, and out of loyalty to her mother, that's exactly what Jennifer did. She wrote her engagement announcement, never mentioning her father.

Jennifer later regretted that decision, and wished that she had done things differently. She wished she had consulted an impartial party as to how the announcement could be written. She wished she had discussed it with her father. She had hurt his feelings, she knew, and that could not be undone.

Newspaper Engagement Announcement

Having a divorce in the family can mean that composing your announcement for the newspaper will take extra time and care. Being sensitive to the feelings of parents and stepparents early will get you off to a good start in your wedding preparations.

The announcement can appear in several newspapers—the hometowns of the bride and groom, the town in which they are currently living, the towns of all divorced parents, and the towns of grandparents. The bride usually assumes the responsibility of sending the information and photographs to appropriate newspapers.

You may request a publication date on the top of the announcement information, but newspapers usually reserve the right to print announcements as space permits, and to edit content according to their style. The following pages contain some specific guidelines for brides and grooms with divorced parents as well as some general guidelines for announcing your engagement.

General Guidelines

• The formal, traditional way for a divorced mother to announce the engagement is to use her maiden and married name (Mrs. Clark Jones). However, many mothers prefer to use their first name, maiden name, and married name (Mrs. Amanda Clark Jones).

- If the bride's mother has remarried and she and the bride's father are announcing the engagement, the bride may choose to use her last name in the announcement for clarification.

- If the bride's mother has remarried and she alone or she and her husband are announcing the engagement, the bride should use her last name in the announcement.

- If both of the bride's parents have remarried and all four are announcing the engagement together, the bride should use her last name.

- If the groom's parents are divorced, follow the same guidelines.

- The newspaper announcement is usually made two or three months before the date of the wedding, although the announcement can appear up to a year before the wedding date, or as close as a week before.

- Check with local newspapers for specific rules and requirements, but make sure that you send the engagement information several weeks before you wish the announcement to be published. Address information to the society editor or lifestyle editor of the newspaper, and include a daytime telephone number, and even a backup number, so that information can be verified.

- If the newspaper publishes photographs, you must submit a black-and-white glossy picture when you submit the written information. Some newspapers print pictures of brides only. Others accept photographs of brides or couples. Check with all newspapers, and decide which you prefer if either type is allowed.

- The city is mentioned in an announcement only when it is not the same as the dateline, which is the city from which the announcement is being issued. When submitting your information to the newspaper, however, list *all* cities for clarification. Let the newspaper edit to suit its style.

- If you are having an engagement party, your announcement should appear in the newspaper the following day, or as close to that date as possible.

- The announcement is usually made by the bride's parents, or her immediate family, even when the announcement is made in the groom's hometown newspaper.

- Engraved or printed engagement announcements should not be sent. The engagement should be announced at an engagement party and/or in the newspaper.

- In the unhappy event that there is a recent death in either family, or a member of the family is seriously ill, it is considered in poor taste to make a public engagement announcement. Instead, the family can spread the news by word of mouth. An announcement can follow after some weeks have passed.

Engagement Announcement Examples

If the bride's parents are divorced, traditionally the bride's mother makes the announcement, but the bride's father's name is included. However, there are situations which make it more difficult to decide how to word the announcement. The examples in this chapter give many choices, depending on individual circumstances. Look through the list below to select the situation that best applies to your particular case. Most brides choose to use example 1, 2, 3, or 4. If the groom's parents are divorced, similar wording is followed in the engagement announcement.

1. *Bride's mother not remarried and making announcement alone; bride's father should be mentioned*

2. *Bride's mother remarried and making announcement alone; bride's father should be mentioned*

3. *Bride's mother not remarried; bride's mother and father making announcement together*

4. *Bride's mother remarried; bride's mother and father making announcement together*

5. *Bride's mother and stepfather making announcement; bride's father may be mentioned*

6. *Both bride's parents remarried and bride close to all; all four making announcement together*

7. *Bride's father making announcement alone; bride's mother may be mentioned*

8. *Bride's father and stepmother making announcement; bride's mother may be mentioned*

9. *Bride's mother deceased (parents divorced before mother's death); father remarried and father alone or father and stepmother making announcement; deceased mother should be mentioned*

10. *Bride's father deceased (parents divorced before father's death); mother remarried and mother alone or mother and stepfather making announcement; deceased father should be mentioned*

11. *Bride's mother or father deceased (parents divorced before death); bride raised by aunt and uncle who are making announcement; deceased parent should be mentioned*

12. *Bride and groom making their own announcement*

13. *Bride's parents separated*

1. Bride's mother not remarried and making announcement alone; bride's father should be mentioned

Mrs. Amanda Clark Jones of Atlanta announces the engagement of her daughter, Jennifer Lee, to Mr. Gordon Floyd Bland, son of Mr. and Mrs. David Calhoun Bland of Richmond, Virginia. Miss Jones is also the daughter of Mr. Steven Riley Jones of Macon, Georgia.

Miss Jones is the granddaughter of Mr. and Mrs. John William Clark of Atlanta and the late Mr. and Mrs. Steven Riley Jones, Sr., of Macon. Mr. Bland is the grandson of Mrs. Conrad Thomas Smith of Richmond and the late Mr. Smith and the late Mr. and Mrs. Jackson Floyd Bland.

Miss Jones was graduated from the Westminster School of Atlanta and the University of Georgia. She is employed with the Fulton County School System. Mr. Bland was graduated from Episcopal High School in Alexandria, Virginia, and the University of Virginia. He is associated with the Commonwealth National Bank of Virginia.

An August wedding is planned.

Announcement refers to *her* daughter.

2. Bride's mother remarried and making announcement alone; bride's father should be mentioned

Mrs. Glenn Richards Simpson of Atlanta announces the engagement of her daughter, Jennifer Lee Jones, to Mr. Gordon Floyd Bland, son of Mr. and Mrs. David Calhoun Bland of Richmond, Virginia. Miss Jones is also the daughter of Mr. Steven Riley Jones of Macon.

Miss Jones is the granddaughter of Mr. and Mrs. John William Clark of Atlanta and the late Mr. and Mrs. Steven Riley Jones, Sr., of Macon. Mr. Bland is the grandson of Mrs. Conrad Thomas Smith of Richmond and the late Mr. Smith and the late Mr. and Mrs. Jackson Floyd Bland.

Miss Jones was graduated from the Westminster School of Atlanta and the University of Georgia. She is employed with the Fulton County School System. Mr. Bland was graduated from Episcopal High School in Alexandria, Virginia, and the University of Virginia. He is associated with the Commonwealth National Bank of Virginia.

An August wedding is planned.

Announcement refers to *her* daughter, and bride's full name is used.

3. *Bride's mother not remarried; bride's mother and father making announcement together*

Mrs. Amanda Clark Jones of Atlanta and Mr. Steven Riley Jones of Macon announce the engagement of their daughter, Jennifer Lee, to Mr. Gordon Floyd Bland, son of Mr. and Mrs. David Calhoun Bland of Richmond, Virginia.

Miss Jones is the granddaughter of Mr. and Mrs. John William Clark of Atlanta and the late Mr. and Mrs. Steven Riley Jones, Sr., of Macon. Mr. Bland is the grandson of Mrs. Conrad Thomas Smith of Richmond and the late Mr. Smith and the late Mr. and Mrs. Jackson Floyd Bland.

Miss Jones was graduated from the Westminster School of Atlanta and the University of Georgia. She is employed with the Fulton County School System. Mr. Bland was graduated from Episcopal High School in Alexandria, Virginia, and the University of Virginia. He is associated with the Commonwealth National Bank of Virginia.

An August wedding is planned.

Announcement refers to *their* daughter.

4. *Bride's mother remarried; bride's mother and father making announcement together*

Mrs. Glenn Richards Simpson of Atlanta and Mr. Steven Riley Jones of Macon announce the engagement of their daughter, Jennifer Lee Jones, to Mr. Gordon Floyd Bland, son of Mr. and Mrs. David Calhoun Bland of Richmond, Virginia.

Miss Jones is the granddaughter of Mr. and Mrs. John William Clark of Atlanta and the late Mr. and Mrs. Steven Riley Jones, Sr., of Macon. Mr. Bland is the grandson of Mrs. Conrad Thomas Smith of Richmond and the late Mr. Smith and the late Mr. and Mrs. Jackson Floyd Bland.

Miss Jones was graduated from the Westminster School of Atlanta and the University of Georgia. She is employed with the Fulton County School System. Mr. Bland was graduated from Episcopal High School in Alexandria, Virginia, and the University of Virginia. He is associated with the Commonwealth National Bank of Virginia.

An August wedding is planned.

Announcement refers to *their* daughter, and bride's full name is used.

5. *Bride's mother and stepfather making announcement; bride's father may be mentioned*

Mr. and Mrs. Glenn Richards Simpson of Atlanta announce the engagement of her daughter, Jennifer Lee Jones, to Mr. Gordon Floyd Bland, son of Mr. and Mrs. David Calhoun Bland of Richmond, Virginia. Miss Jones is also the daughter of Mr. Steven Riley Jones of Macon.

Miss Jones is the granddaughter of Mr. and Mrs. John William Clark of Atlanta and the late Mr. and Mrs. Steven Riley Jones, Sr., of Macon. Mr. Bland is the grandson of Mrs. Conrad Thomas Smith of Richmond and the late Mr. Smith and the late Mr. and Mrs. Jackson Floyd Bland.

Miss Jones was graduated from the Westminster School of Atlanta and the University of Georgia. She is employed with the Fulton County School System. Mr. Bland was graduated from Episcopal High School in Alexandria, Virginia, and the University of Virginia. He is associated with the Commonwealth National Bank of Virginia.

An August wedding is planned.

Announcement refers to *her* daughter. If the bride has known only her stepfather and chooses for her mother and stepfather to announce her engagement, the announcement may refer to *their* daughter and her father would not be mentioned.

6. *Both bride's parents remarried and bride close to all; all four making announcement together*

Mr. and Mrs. Glenn Richards Simpson of Atlanta and Mr. and Mrs. Steven Riley Jones of Macon announce the engagement of Jennifer Lee Jones to Mr. Gordon Floyd Bland, son of Mr. and Mrs. David Calhoun Bland of Richmond, Virginia.

Miss Jones is the granddaughter of Mr. and Mrs. John William Clark of Atlanta and the late Mr. and Mrs. Steven Riley Jones, Sr., of Macon. Mr. Bland is the grandson of Mrs. Conrad Thomas Smith of Richmond and the late Mr. Smith and the late Mr. and Mrs. Jackson Floyd Bland.

Miss Jones was graduated from the Westminster School of Atlanta and the University of Georgia. She is employed with the Fulton County School System. Mr. Bland was graduated from Episcopal High School in Alexandria, Virginia, and the University of Virginia. He is associated with the Commonwealth National Bank of Virginia.

An August wedding is planned.

Announcement omits the wording *their daughter,* and bride's full name is used.

7. *Bride's father making announcement alone; bride's mother may be mentioned.*

Mr. Steven Riley Jones of Macon announces the engagement of his daughter, Jennifer Lee, to Mr. Gordon Floyd Bland, son of Mr. and Mrs. David Calhoun Bland of Richmond, Virginia. Miss Jones is also the daughter of Mrs. Amanda Clark Jones of Atlanta.

Miss Jones is the granddaughter of Mr. and Mrs. John William Clark of Atlanta and the late Mr. and Mrs. Steven Riley Jones, Sr., of Macon. Mr. Bland is the grandson of Mrs. Conrad Thomas Smith of Richmond and the late Mr. Smith and the late Mr. and Mrs. Jackson Floyd Bland.

Miss Jones was graduated from the Westminster School of Atlanta and the University of Georgia. She is employed with the Fulton County School System. Mr. Bland was graduated from Episcopal High School in Alexandria, Virginia, and the University of Virginia. He is associated with the Commonwealth National Bank of Virginia.

An August wedding is planned.

Announcement refers to *his* daughter, and bride's mother may be mentioned.

8. *Bride's father and stepmother making announcement; bride's mother may be mentioned*

Mrs. and Mrs. Steven Riley Jones of Macon announce the engagement of his daughter, Jennifer Lee, to Mr. Gordon Floyd Bland, son of Mr. and Mrs. David Calhoun Bland of Richmond, Virginia. Miss Jones is also the daughter of Mrs. Amanda Clark Jones of Atlanta.

Miss Jones is the granddaughter of Mr. and Mrs. John William Clark of Atlanta and the late Mr. and Mrs. Steven Riley Jones, Sr., of Macon. Mr. Bland is the grandson of Mrs. Conrad Thomas Smith of Richmond and the late Mr. Smith and the late Mr. and Mrs. Jackson Floyd Bland.

Miss Jones was graduated from the Westminster School of Atlanta and the University of Georgia. She is employed with the Fulton County School System. Mr. Bland was graduated from Episcopal High School in Alexandria, Virginia, and the University of Virginia. He is associated with the Commonwealth National Bank of Virginia.

An August wedding is planned.

Announcement refers to *his* daughter. If the bride has known only her stepmother and chooses for her father and stepmother to announce her engagement, the announcement may refer to *their* daughter and her mother would not be mentioned.

9. *Bride's mother deceased (parents divorced before mother's death); father remarried and father alone or father and stepmother making announcement; deceased mother should be mentioned*

Mr. Steven Riley Jones of Macon announces the engagement of his daughter, Jennifer Lee, to Mr. Gordon Floyd Bland, son of Mr. and Mrs. David Calhoun Bland of Richmond, Virginia. Miss Jones is also the daughter of the late Mrs. Amanda Clark Jones of Atlanta.

Miss Jones is the granddaughter of Mr. and Mrs. John William Clark of Atlanta and the late Mr. and Mrs. Steven Riley Jones, Sr., of Macon. Mr. Bland is the grandson of Mrs. Conrad Thomas Smith of Richmond and the late Mr. Smith and the late Mr. and Mrs. Jackson Floyd Bland.

Miss Jones was graduated from the Westminster School of Atlanta and the University of Georgia. She is employed with the Fulton County School System. Mr. Bland was graduated from Episcopal High School in Alexandria, Virginia, and the University of Virginia. He is associated with the Commonwealth National Bank of Virginia.

An August wedding is planned.

Announcement refers to *his* daughter. If the bride is close to her stepmother and chooses for her father and stepmother to make the announcement, it would read "Mr. and Mrs. Steven Riley Jones" and refer to *his* daughter. The bride's deceased mother should be mentioned.

10. *Bride's father deceased (parents divorced before father's death); mother remarried and mother alone or mother and stepfather making announcement; deceased father should be mentioned*

Mrs. Glenn Richards Simpson of Atlanta announces the engagement of her daughter, Jennifer Lee Jones, to Mr. Gordon Floyd Bland, son of Mr. and Mrs. David Calhoun Bland of Richmond, Virginia. Miss Jones is also the daughter of the late Mr. Steven Riley Jones of Macon.

Miss Jones is the granddaughter of Mr. and Mrs. John William Clark of Atlanta and the late Mr. and Mrs. Steven Riley Jones, Sr., of Macon. Mr. Bland is the grandson of Mrs. Conrad Thomas Smith of Richmond and the late Mr. Smith and the late Mr. and Mrs. Jackson Floyd Bland.

Miss Jones was graduated from the Westminster School of Atlanta and the University of Georgia. She is employed with the Fulton County School System. Mr. Bland was graduated from Episcopal High School in Alexandria, Virginia, and the University of Virginia. He is associated with the Commonwealth National Bank of Virginia.

An August wedding is planned.

Announcement refers to *her* daughter, and bride's full name must be used. If the bride is close to her stepfather and chooses for her mother and stepfather to make the announcement, it would read "Mr. and Mrs. Glenn Richards Simpson" and refer to *her* daughter. The bride's deceased father should be mentioned.

11. *Bride's mother or father deceased (parents divorced before death); bride raised by aunt and uncle who are making announcement; deceased parent should be mentioned*

Mr. and Mrs. Charles Murray Smith of Atlanta announce the engagement of their niece, Jennifer Lee Jones, to Mr. Gordon Floyd Bland, son of Mr. and Mrs. David Calhoun Bland of Richmond, Virginia. Miss Jones is the daughter of the late Mrs. Amanda Clark Jones of Atlanta and of Mr. Steven Riley Jones of Macon.

Miss Jones is the granddaughter of Mr. and Mrs. John William Clark of Atlanta and the late Mr. and Mrs. Steven Riley Jones, Sr., of Macon. Mr. Bland is the grandson of Mrs. Conrad Thomas Smith of Richmond and the late Mr. Smith and the late Mr. and Mrs. Jackson Floyd Bland.

Miss Jones was graduated from the Westminster School of Atlanta and the University of Georgia. She is employed with the Fulton County School System. Mr. Bland was graduated from Episcopal High School in Alexandria, Virginia, and the University of Virginia. He is associated with the Commonwealth National Bank of Virginia.

An August wedding is planned.

Announcement refers to *their* niece, and bride's full name is used. The bride's deceased parent should be mentioned. Her living parent may be mentioned if the bride chooses to do so.

12. Bride and groom making their own announcement

When the bride and groom find that family relations are too strained, they may choose to announce their own engagement.

Miss Jennifer Lee Jones and Mr. Gordon Floyd Bland announce their engagement. Miss Jones is the daughter of Mrs. Amanda Clark Jones of Atlanta and Mr. Steven Riley Jones of Macon. Mr. Bland is the son of Mr. and Mrs. David Calhoun Bland of Richmond, Virginia.

Miss Jones is the granddaughter of Mr. and Mrs. John William Clark of Atlanta and the late Mr. and Mrs. Steven Riley Jones, Sr., of Macon. Mr. Bland is the grandson of Mrs. Conrad Thomas Smith of Richmond and the late Mr. Smith and the late Mr. and Mrs. Jackson Floyd Bland.

Miss Jones was graduated from the Westminster School of Atlanta and the University of Georgia. She is employed with the Fulton County School System. Mr. Bland was graduated from Episcopal High School in Alexandria, Virginia, and the University of Virginia. He is associated with the Commonwealth National Bank of Virginia.

An August wedding is planned.

Here is an example of a more impersonal way for the couple to make their own announcement.

The engagement of Jennifer Lee Jones, daughter of Mrs. Amanda Clark Jones of Atlanta and Mr. Steven Riley Jones of Macon, is announced to Mr. Gordon Floyd Bland, son of Mr. and Mrs. David Calhoun Bland of Richmond, Virginia.

Miss Jones is the granddaughter of Mr. and Mrs. John William Clark of Atlanta and the late Mr. and Mrs. Steven Riley Jones, Sr., of Macon. Mr. Bland is the grandson of Mrs. Conrad Thomas Smith of Richmond and the late Mr. Smith and the late Mr. and Mrs. Jackson Floyd Bland.

Miss Jones was graduated from the Westminster School of Atlanta and the University of Georgia. She is employed with the Fulton County School System. Mr. Bland was graduated from Episcopal High School in Alexandria, Virginia, and the University of Virginia. He is associated with the Commonwealth National Bank of Virginia.

An August wedding is planned.

13. Bride's parents separated

When the bride's parents are legally separated but not divorced, the announcement is made by the parent with whom the bride lives or has lived. This is usually the mother, who continues to use her husband's name. Parents who are separated may also announce the engagement as Mr. and Mrs.

Mrs. Steven Riley Jones of Atlanta announces the engagement of her daughter, Jennifer Lee, to Mr. Gordon Floyd Bland, son of Mr. and Mrs. David Calhoun Bland of Richmond, Virginia. Miss Jones is also the daughter of Mr. Steven Riley Jones.

Miss Jones is the granddaughter of Mr. and Mrs. John William Clark of Atlanta and the late Mr. and Mrs. Steven Riley Jones, Sr., of Macon. Mr. Bland is the grandson of Mrs. Conrad Thomas Smith of Richmond and the late Mr. Smith and the late Mr. and Mrs. Jackson Floyd Bland.

Miss Jones was graduated from the Westminster School of Atlanta and the University of Georgia. She is employed with the Fulton County School System. Mr. Bland was graduated from Episcopal High School in Alexandria, Virginia, and the University of Virginia. He is associated with the Commonwealth National Bank of Virginia.

An August wedding is planned.

Announcement refers to *her* daughter.

5

Invitations

It was becoming increasingly obvious to Jennifer that her father wasn't going to help financially with her wedding. Her mother, Amanda, wasn't surprised. She and Jennifer's father had divorced when Jennifer and her brother were small, and she knew that her ex-husband historically had paid for nothing more than the divorce decree required. In exasperation, Amanda finally told her daughter: "Jennifer, it's time you talked candidly with your father. Find out exactly what he is willing to pay for, so that we can go ahead and plan this wedding. We're running out of time."

So Jennifer asked her father outright what he intended to spend on the wedding. "You aren't doing it the way I think you should, so why don't you just let your mother pay for it? I'll still participate, and I'll give you away. But I won't pay," he said.

Jennifer cried most of the next day, but then announced to her mother that she was ready to pick out the invitations. They went to a printing company with experienced personnel. Because Jennifer did not want to leave anyone out, she asked the consultant to make up a sample invitation including both sets of parents—Jennifer's father and his wife, and Jennifer's mother and her husband. After the consultant wrote out a sample invitation, she asked, "Are both sets of your parents sharing in the costs?" Jennifer dropped her eyes and shook her head. The consultant said, "Then I must tell you that to be correct, the invitation really should include only the names of the people who are paying for the wedding. They are the hosts, and they are issuing the invitation."

After a quiet moment, Jennifer reached her hand across the table, turned the invitation around to face her, picked up a pencil, and crossed out the names of her father and stepmother, since he had refused to help with her wedding costs.

The decision had been made. It was difficult, but it was correct. And from that point on, Jennifer's mother and stepfather became the hosts, and her father and stepmother became invited guests. And who could complain? Jennifer had given her father the choice, and he had chosen his position.

Selecting the Invitation

The style of the invitation should be in keeping with the type of wedding that is planned. It will set the tone for the rest of the events to follow, and will become a treasured keepsake for the bride and groom, their families, and close friends. Make it something to be cherished in years to come!

The bride will want to begin by going to a reputable stationer, one with experienced personnel. If the bride has a wedding consultant, she or he may recommend stationers. Otherwise, consult a bridal shop or a jeweler for suggestions. In cases involving divorced parents, experienced stationers can pass along their knowledge, their sense of good taste, and the rules of etiquette to help the bride with the wording of her invitation.

A wedding may be formal, semiformal, or informal, and the invitation should reflect that choice. The formality of the wedding depends on the location of the ceremony and reception, the size of the wedding party, and the number of guests to be invited. For example, up to seventy-five people could be considered an informal wedding, seventy-five to two hundred a semiformal wedding, and more than two hundred a formal wedding. However, even a small wedding can be a very formal affair. The formality or informality of the wedding—and the invitation—depends on what the bride and groom want.

For small or informal weddings, engraved or printed invitations are not necessary. The bride or her mother may call, or write personal invitations. If writing, use ivory or white fold-over paper of the finest stock affordable. The bride may choose the traditional wording that would be used on an engraved invitation, spaced accordingly. Or she may write an informal note.

If, however, the wedding will be larger, there are several types of invitations from which to choose, from very traditional to original custom designs. Brides and grooms can select from a variety of papers, from formal thick white or ivory to less formal parchment.

Regardless of the size of the wedding, the wording on the invitation is basically the same. However, in cases where there are divorced parents, there is some leeway to accommodate the special circumstances. We have tried to include many of these situations in this chapter.

Once the wording is determined, the size and style of the typeface is selected. This, along with the selection of the paper, will determine the overall appearance of the invitation.

The invitations should be ordered early enough to allow time for engraving or printing, addressing, and mailing. They should be sent out four to six weeks before the wedding.

Order more invitations than needed—the cost of an additional twenty-five or fifty invitations ordered at the onset is minimal. Order extra envelopes to allow for inevitable mistakes. The bride may even want to pick up the envelopes in advance of the invitations so that she can be addressing them while the invitations are being engraved or printed.

The Invitation Style

THE STOCK

When the bride visits her stationer, he or she will show her the variety of grades and shades of paper from which she may select. Ivory, soft cream, and white are the most preferred shades. The heavier the stock, the more luxurious—and expensive—the invitation. Choose the heaviest weight you can afford. The stock can be plain or paneled with a blind embossed border.

Some of the most beautiful invitations are those engraved on paper made from cotton. The cotton fiber makes the invitations feel smooth and rich, and the paper will last forever.

THE LETTERING

If the bride chooses a plain paper, she may want to go with a script lettering style. If she chooses a paneled paper, she may want to pick a print style, which looks better contained inside the paneling.

There are many lettering styles to choose from, and the stationer will tell her about them all. Basically, she should choose something that she likes and that fits the formality of her wedding. We suggest that the bride choose something traditional and classic rather than something trendy, which will age badly. She will want to look back on her selection in years to come and congratulate herself on her good taste! Shaded Roman, Antique Roman, and Script are simple styles that come highly recommended.

THE INK

Black ink is correct on all formal invitations. However, if the bride chooses a thick lettering style, and is having it printed on white paper, she may choose a dark gray ink for clarity. The stationer will be glad to help with this decision.

A COAT OF ARMS

If the bride's family has a coat of arms, this is one of the few chances they will have to use it. It can be embossed without color at the top center of the invitation. It may take several months to order and receive the coat of arms engraving die if the family does not already have one, so that delay needs to be figured into the invitation timetable.

ENGRAVING AND THERMOGRAPHY

Engraved invitations are the most formal, the most beautiful, and the most expensive. They can be distinguished from other forms of printing by the sharp lines and the impression on the back of the paper caused by the pressure from the copper plate. Thermography, a method of raised printing, gives a similar look and is less expensive. Many invitations today are printed by thermography.

The Guest List

The bride and groom should begin to compile their guest list as soon as they become engaged. To help organize the list, put each person or couple on a separate 3-by-5-inch index card with the complete name and address. Typically, the bride's family and the groom's family each invites half the guests, unless one family knows in advance that they will have fewer guests. "Guest proportions" should be agreed upon as soon as possible. This is particularly important when parents are divorced. So discuss the list with all parents involved. Stepfamilies should be included if at all possible.

The groom's family should give their guest list to the bride so that she can combine it with her list and determine the number of invitations that will be needed. Sometimes the list will need to be shortened, with help from both families.

In order to make addressing of the invitations simpler (see "Guidelines for Addressing Invitations," page 85), the bride should request that each person provide complete names just as they will appear on the envelope, e.g., Mrs. John William Jones, not Mrs. J. W. Jones. Also include complete addresses with zip codes.

When compiling the guest list, children under eighteen should be included with their parents, and their names added to the inner envelope. Traditionally, anyone over the age of eighteen should be sent a separate invitation.

For a large, formal wedding, invitations should be sent to all close friends and relatives, even those who live far away and cannot possibly attend the wedding. The guest list will include all relatives of the bride and groom, all close friends of both families, neighbors of both families, and business associates of the bride, groom, and their parents. Wedding invitations are never sent to casual business or social acquaintances.

Invitations should be sent to the guests on the list, as well as to the groom's immediate family, the wedding party, and their spouses or dates. Make sure to save an invitation for the bride and groom!

Wording the Invitation

How to word the invitation may be one of the most important decisions the bride makes while planning her wedding, so she should gather all the available information, think through what she wants to say, and *ask* for her parents' input. Remember, there are many emotions involved when dealing with divorced parents and their spouses. Remember, too, the invitation is being sent to people they care about and respect, as well as to the bride's and groom's friends.

The bride may find herself in a situation, however, in which her parents cannot agree on whose name or names will appear on the invitation. She needs to handle this predicament with concern for everyone's feelings. Consideration must be given to the parent with whom the bride lives, or lived while she was growing up, as well as to the parent who is paying for the wedding. Traditionally, a bride's father pays for his daughter's wedding, but her mother should be included on the invitation if she is helping financially as much as she can. If either parent can't afford to help financially and refuses to do so, then his or her name should not be included on the invitation.

When the bride's parents are divorced, there are many different ways to word the invitation. Everyone's situation is different. The examples in this chapter illustrate some of the more common situations that may occur.

Rules for Traditional Wording

- All names are spelled out in full, without nicknames or initials.

- "Doctor" is written in full, unless the name that follows is long. "Mr." and "Jr." are preferred, although "Junior" may be used.

- Commas after days of the week and periods after abbreviations such as "Mr.," "Jr.," and "St. Anne's" are the only punctuation used.

- In a divorce situation when both parents are hosting the wedding, the word *and* may or may not be used between their names. (See examples later in this chapter.)

- The traditional wording on all wedding invitations reads: "requests the honour [with *honour* spelled the English way, with a *u*] of your presence at the marriage . . ."

- The bride's surname is not listed unless it is different from that of her parents.

- The date of the wedding is spelled out rather than written as a numeral: "Saturday, the fifth of November."

- The year is spelled out—"nineteen hundred and ninety-two" or "one thousand nine hundred and ninety-two"—following the date. If you wish, the year may be eliminated.

- The time of the wedding is "six o'clock," not 6:00 P.M. Half hours are "half after seven" instead of "seven-thirty" or "half past seven." For clarification, you may add "in the morning," "in the afternoon," or "in the evening" after the time.

- No words are capitalized except proper nouns—people's names and titles, place names, names of days and months.

- The church's address is not needed if the invitation is issued in a small town or city. In larger cities, where everyone may not know the church, the address is helpful. The city and state are always included. If the street address is long, numerals may be used.

- If the hosts ask for a response, "Please respond," "The favor of a reply is requested," "R.S.V.P.," and "R.s.v.p." are all correct.

Invitation Examples

The following invitation examples illustrate different ways to word the invitation according to the bride's situation. Look through all of the examples listed below to select the one which most likely applies to your particular case. Each of the examples listed below are expanded considerably in this chapter.

1. *Neither of bride's parents remarried and issuing invitation together*

2. *Bride's mother remarried*
   a. Bride's mother and father issuing invitation
   b. Bride's mother and stepfather issuing invitation
   c. Bride's mother, stepfather, and father issuing invitation

3. *Bride's father remarried*
   a. Bride's father and stepmother issuing invitation
   b. Bride's mother, father, and stepmother issuing invitation

4. *Both bride's parents remarried and all four issuing invitation together*

5. *Bride's mother issuing invitation to wedding and father issuing invitation to reception*

6. *Bride's mother deceased (parents divorced before mother's death); father may or may not be remarried; bride chooses for her father to issue invitation*

7. *Bride's mother deceased (parents divorced before mother's death); father remarried; father and stepmother issuing invitation*

8. *Bride's father deceased (parents divorced before father's death); mother may or may not be remarried; mother issuing invitation*

9. *Bride's aunt and uncle or very close friends issuing invitation*

10. *Bride and groom issuing invitation*

11. *Bride's parents separated*

1. Neither of bride's parents remarried and issuing invitation together

If the bride's parents are divorced and both names are to appear on the invitation (because they share in the wedding expenses and are cohosts), the name of the bride's mother appears on the first line and the name of the bride's father appears on the second line.

Mrs. Amanda Clark Jones

and

Mr. Steven Riley Jones

request the honour of your presence

at the marriage of their daughter

Jennifer Lee

to

Mr. Gordon Floyd Bland

on Saturday, the fourth of August

Nineteen hundred and ninety

at two o'clock

First United Methodist Church

Savannah, Georgia

Invitation refers to *their* daughter. The word *and* may be omitted.

On formal correspondence, a divorced woman traditionally used her maiden name and her last name rather than her first name: for example, Mrs. Clark Jones. Although this is technically correct, many divorcées today choose to use their first name along with their maiden name and married name, because few people would know them by the traditional name. Example: Mrs. Amanda Clark Jones. Occasionally, a woman may also revert to her maiden name, although this does not happen often when she has children, who would then have last names that are different from hers. Using only Mrs. Amanda Jones (the given name and her married last name) is not acceptable on a formal invitation.

Therefore, it is now acceptable for a divorcee to send out her daughter's invitations as:

Mrs. Clark Jones

or

Mrs. Amanda Clark Jones

2. Bride's mother remarried
  a. Bride's mother and father issuing invitation

When the bride's mother has remarried and the mother and father of the bride are sharing the expenses, the invitation should read:

Mrs. Glenn Richards Simpson

and

Mr. Stephen Riley Jones
request the honour of your presence
at the marriage of their daughter
Jennifer Lee Jones

to

Mr. Gordon Floyd Bland
on Saturday, the fourth of August
Nineteen hundred and ninety
at two o'clock
First United Methodist church
Savannah, Georgia

Invitation refers to *their* daughter, and may show bride's full name. The word *and* may be omitted.

b. Bride's mother and stepfather issuing invitation

When the bride's mother has remarried and she and her husband are paying for the wedding, the invitations are worded:

Mr. and Mrs. Glenn Richards Simpson
request the honour of your presence
at the marriage of her daughter
Jennifer Lee Jones
to
Mr. Gordon Floyd Bland
on Saturday, the fourth of August
Nineteen hundred and ninety
at two o'clock
First United Methodist Church
Savannah, Georgia

Invitation refers to *her* daughter, and must show bride's full name.

If the bride's father has no part in her life, and her stepfather has brought her up, the invitation reads:

Mr. and Mrs. Glenn Richards Simpson

request the honour of your presence

at the marriage of their daughter

Jennifer Lee Jones

to

Mr. Gordon Floyd Bland

on Saturday, the fourth of August

Nineteen hundred and ninety

at two o'clock

First United Methodist Church

Savannah, Georgia

Invitation refers to *their* daughter, and must show bride's full name.

c. Bride's mother, stepfather, and father issuing invitation

If the bride is close to her father and her stepfather, both of their names can appear on the invitation. In this case, the mother's and stepfather's names appear first. The invitation may read this way:

Mr. and Mrs. Glenn Richards Simpson

and

Mr. Steven Riley Jones

request the honour of your presence

at the marriage of

Jennifer Lee Jones

to

Mr. Gordon Floyd Bland

on Saturday, the fourth of August

Nineteen hundred and ninety

at two o'clock

First United Methodist Church

123 Abercorn Street

Savannah, Georgia

The words *their daughter* are omitted, and the bride's full name is used. The word *and* may be omitted.

3. Bride's father remarried
   a. Bride's father and stepmother issuing invitation

If the bride's father and stepmother are sending the invitations, they would read:

> *Mr. and Mrs. Steven Riley Jones*
> *request the honour of your presence*
> *at the marriage of his daughter*
> *Jennifer Lee*
>
> *to*
>
> *Mr. Gordon Floyd Bland*
> *on Saturday, the fourth of August*
> *Nineteen hundred and ninety*
> *at two o'clock*
> *First United Methodist Church*
> *Savannah, Georgia*

Invitation refers to *his* daughter, and uses bride's first names only. If the bride and stepmother are not close, the stepmother should have the courtesy to request that her name be omitted from the invitation.

b. Bride's mother, father, and stepmother issuing invitation

If the bride is close to her mother and her stepmother, both their names can appear on the invitation—even if the bride's mother can help financially with the wedding and reception in only a small way. In this case, the mother's name should appear first. The invitation may read this way:

Mrs. Amanda Clark Jones

and

Mr. and Mrs. Steven Riley Jones

request the honour of your presence

at the marriage of

Jennifer Lee Jones

to

Mr. Gordon Floyd Bland

on Saturday, the fourth of August

Nineteen hundred and ninety

at two o'clock

First United Methodist Church

Savannah, Georgia

The words *their daughter* are omitted, and bride's full name is used. The word *and* may be omitted.

4. Both bride's parents remarried and all four issuing invitation together

In the event that relations between the bride's divorced parents are so friendly that they share the wedding expenses and act as cohosts, both couples' names may appear on the invitation. The bride's mother's name appears first.

Mr. and Mrs. Glenn Richards Simpson

and

Mr. and Mrs. Steven Riley Jones

request the honour of your presence

at the marriage of

Jennifer Lee Jones

to

Mr. Gordon Floyd Bland

on Saturday, the fourth of August

Nineteen hundred and ninety

at two o'clock

First United Methodist Church

Savannah, Georgia

The words *their daughter* are omitted, and bride's full name is used. The word *and* may be omitted.

5. Bride's mother issuing invitation to wedding and father issuing invitation to reception

In some cases, relations between divorced parents are so strained that they choose to distinctly divide the expenses, with one paying for the wedding and the other paying for the reception. In this instance, the bride's mother issues the wedding invitation and the bride's father issues the reception invitation (or vice versa). This may also apply if either or both parents have remarried. The invitation should read:

Mrs. Amanda Clark Jones

requests the honour of your presence

at the marriage of her daughter

Jennifer Lee

to

Mr. Gordon Floyd Bland

on Saturday, the fourth of August

Nineteen hundred and ninety

at two o'clock

First United Methodist Church

Savannah, Georgia

Invitation refers to *her* daughter.

The reception card should read:

Mr. Stephen Riley Jones
requests the pleasure of your company
at the wedding reception
Saturday, the fourth of August
at three o'clock
Forest Heights Country Club

R.S.V.P.
24 Fairfield Lane
Savannah, Georgia 31411

The bride's stepmother's name may also appear.

6. *Bride's mother deceased (parents divorced before mother's death); father may or may not be remarried; bride chooses for her father to issue invitation*

Mr. Stephen Riley Jones

requests the honour of your presence

at the marriage of his daughter

Jennifer Lee

to

Mr. Gordon Floyd Bland

on Saturday, the fourth of August

Nineteen hundred and ninety

at two o'clock

First United Methodist church

Savannah, Georgia

Invitation refers to *his* daughter, and uses bride's first names only. If the bride and stepmother are not close, the stepmother should have the courtesy to request that her name be omitted from the invitation.

7. *Bride's mother deceased (parents divorced before mother's death); father remarried; father and stepmother issuing invitation*

Mr. and Mrs. Steven Riley Jones
request the honour of your presence
at the marriage of his daughter
Jennifer Lee

to

Mr. Gordon Floyd Bland
on Saturday, the fourth of August
Nineteen hundred and ninety
at two o'clock
First United Methodist Church
Savannah, Georgia

Invitation refers to *his* daughter, and uses bride's first names only.

8. *Bride's father deceased (parents divorced before father's death); mother may or may not be remarried; mother issuing invitation*

Mrs. Amanda Clark Jones

requests the honour of your presence

at the marriage of her daughter

Jennifer Lee

to

Mr. Gordon Floyd Bland

on Saturday, the fourth of August

Nineteen hundred and ninety

at two o'clock

First United Methodist Church

Savannah, Georgia

The invitation refers to *her* daughter, and uses bride's first names only.

9. Bride's aunt and uncle or very close friends issuing invitation

Certain circumstances could have occurred to account for the fact that the bride's aunt and uncle or close friends are issuing the invitation.

Mr. and Mrs. Charles Murray Smith

request the honour of your presence

at the marriage of their niece

Jennifer Lee Jones

to

Mr. Gordon Floyd Bland

on Saturday, the fourth of August

Nineteen hundred and ninety

at two o'clock

First United Methodist church

Savannah, Georgia

Invitation refers to *their niece,* and bride's full name is used if aunt and uncle are issuing invitation. If friends are issuing the invitation, *of their niece* would be omitted, and no mention would be made of the relationship to the bride.

10. Bride and groom issuing invitation

Sometimes the bride and groom may decide to issue their own invitation. They may be in a position to finance their own wedding, or may find that issuing the invitation themselves causes the least conflict between family members. In either of those cases, the invitation might read:

Miss Jennifer Lee Jones

and

Mr. Gordon Floyd Bland

request the honour of your presence

at their marriage

on Saturday, the tenth of May

Nineteen hundred and ninety

at two o'clock

First United Methodist Church

Savannah, Georgia

or:

The honour of your presence is requested
at the marriage of
Jennifer Lee Jones

to

Mr. Gordon Floyd Bland
on Saturday, the fourth of August
Nineteen hundred and ninety
at two o'clock
First United Methodist Church
Savannah, Georgia

11. Bride's parents separated

Invitations and announcements are in the name of the parent (or relative) with whom the bride lives or lived—usually the mother, who must use her husband's name, e.g., Mrs. Steven Riley Jones, or her professional name, if she has one, e.g., Amanda Clark Jones.

Parents who are separated but not divorced may issue the invitation as "Mr. and Mrs."

Guidelines for Addressing Invitations

- Invitations should be hand-addressed, preferably in black ink. They should be addressed by someone with a neat, beautiful handwriting, or in calligraphy.

- Use no abbreviations except Mr., Mrs., Ms., Dr., or Jr.

- Symbols should not be used. For example, write out *and* rather than use an ampersand.

- Initials are not acceptable. Write "William," not "W." Omit the initial if you do not know it.

- North, South, East, and West should not be abbreviated.

- Street, Road, Avenue, Boulevard, and Lane should always be written out, not abbreviated.

- States are spelled out in full (for example: Georgia, not GA).

- Figures are used in zip codes and house numbers. Numbered streets are written out. For example: Fourteenth Street, not 14th Street, or One Hundred and Twenty-fifth Street, not 125th Street.

- Avoid "and family" if possible. All children over age eighteen should receive a separate invitation.

- Invitations should be mailed from four to six weeks before the wedding.

- Mail invitations first-class mail, never metered mail.

- Be sure to include a return address on the invitations.

- Wedding announcements are addressed the same as invitations, and should be mailed immediately *after* the wedding.

Addressing the Inner and Outer Envelopes

Most wedding invitations have two separate envelopes, the outer envelope and the inner envelope, which contains the actual invitation. The following guidelines apply to addressing them:

- *To a married couple*
  Outer: Mr. and Mrs. Walter Stuart Brown
  Inner: Mr. and Mrs. Brown

- *To a married couple with children under eighteen*
  Outer: Mr. and Mrs. Walter Stuart Brown
  Inner: Mr. and Mrs. Brown
  Jane and Paul

- *To an unmarried couple at the same address (on a formal invitation, Ms. is accepted, but not preferred)*
  Outer: Miss (or Ms.) Emily Jones
  Mr. John Williams (separate line)
  Inner: Miss (or Ms.) Jones
  Mr. Williams

- *To a single woman (on a formal invitation, Ms. is accepted, but not preferred)*
  Outer: Miss (or Ms.) Emily Jones
  Inner: Miss (or Ms.) Jones

- *To a single man*
  Outer: Mr. John Williams
  Inner: Mr. Williams

- *To a widow, or a separated woman*
  Outer: Mrs. Walter Stuart Brown
  Inner: Mrs. Brown

- *To a divorcée who is still using her former husband's name (on a formal invitation, Ms. is accepted, but not preferred)*

   Outer: Mrs. (or Ms.) Smith Robertson or Mrs. (or Ms.) Barbara Smith Robertson (Smith is her maiden name)

   Inner: Mrs. (or Ms.) Robertson

- *To a married couple when the wife uses her maiden name*

   Outer: Ms. Emily Jones and Mr. John Williams
   (Both names are on the same line)

   Inner: Ms. Jones
   Mr. Williams

   Outer: Dr. Julia Trainer and Dr. Thomas McCrary

   Inner: Dr. Trainer
   Dr. McCrary

- *To a single man or woman and guest*

   Outer: Mr. John Williams

   Inner: Mr. Williams and Guest

- *To a married couple, both doctors*

   Outer: The Doctors Williams

   Inner: The Doctors Williams

Special Titles Used in Addressing

Here are some special titles you may need when addressing your envelopes:

PERSONAGE	OUTER ENVELOPE	INNER ENVELOPE
President of the United States	The President and Mrs. George Herbert Walker Bush	President and Mrs. Bush
U.S. Senator	The Honorable and Mrs. John William Smith	Senator and Mrs. Smith

PERSONAGE	OUTER ENVELOPE	INNER ENVELOPE
U.S. Representative	The Honorable and Mrs. John William Jones	Mr. and Mrs. Jones
Governor	The Honorable and Mrs. John William White	Governor and Mrs. White
Mayor	The Honorable and Mrs. Michael James Green	Mayor and Mrs. Green
Judge	The Honorable and Mrs. Arthur Warner Brown	Judge and Mrs. Brown
Army, Air Force, or Marine Corps	Colonel and Mrs. Joseph Bowers	Colonel and Mrs. Bowers
Navy and Coast Guard	Commander and Mrs. Russell Jordan	Commander and Mrs. Jordan
Clergy, Protestant (with Degree)	The Reverend Dr. and Mrs. Joseph Long	Dr. and Mrs. Long
Clergy, Protestant (without Degree)	The Reverend and Mrs. Frank John Anderson	Mr. and Mrs. Anderson
Bishop	The Most Reverend James Andrews, Bishop of Georgia	Bishop Andrews
Episcopal	The Right Reverend and Mrs. Richard Smith, Bishop of Atlanta	The Right Reverend and Mrs. Smith
Rabbi	Rabbi and Mrs. Arthur Goldstein	Rabbi and Mrs. Goldstein
Cantor	Cantor and Mrs. Stanley Levy	Cantor and Mrs. Levy

If any of the above titles belongs to a woman, address the envelopes as follows:

PERSONAGE	OUTER ENVELOPE	INNER ENVELOPE
Judge	The Honorable Susan Bartram and Mr. Frank Bartram	Judge Bartram Mr. Bartram
Dean	Dr. Joan Winters and Mr. David Winters	Dr. Winters Mr. Winters

Assembling and Mailing Invitation

1. *A single-fold invitation inserted in the inner envelope*

2. *Inserting a single-fold invitation with an enclosure card in the inner envelope*

3. *A twice-folded invitation inserted in the inner envelope*

4. *Inserting a twice-folded invitation with an enclosure card in the inner envelope*

5. *Enclosing a reply card and envelope in the inner enverlope*

6. *Placing the inner envelope in the outer envelope*

Larger, formal invitations should be folded first down the left-hand side with the engraving on the front and nothing on the inside. The invitation is then placed in the inner envelope with the fold side down. (See illustration #1.) If this invitation has insertions, such as pew cards, reception cards, or maps, they are placed in front of the invitation with the reception card next to the invitation, and any other cards in front of that. (See illustration #2.)

A once-folded invitation designed to fit into an envelope approximately half its size will have to be folded a second time, with the engraving inside. (See illustration #3.) All insertions are placed inside the second fold, engraved side up. (See illustration #4.)

When enclosing a reply card with its envelope, the card is not put inside its envelope but placed under the flap, engraved side up. It is then inserted in front of the invitation. (See illustration #5.)

The inner envelope is left unsealed and, with the flap facing away from you, is inserted in the mailing envelope. The inner envelope is placed in the outer envelope so that the guests' names are seen first when the envelope is opened. (See illustration #6.)

Tissues used to be provided by engravers to prevent smudging of the ink. However, with improved engraving and printing, they are not necessary and are sometimes not included. If they are, you may throw them away or leave them in, as you wish.

Weigh the invitation before mailing to ensure proper postage. Appropriate commemorative stamps may be purchased to add a special touch.

Response Cards

Response cards are optional, but convenient for guests. They are also helpful for the bride, as she cannot be expected to know a final count for the reception until she has received responses to her invitation. They should be small cards engraved in the same style as the invitation, and should include a self-addressed envelope, preferably stamped. At the top of the following page is a sample card.

Please respond on or before
June 30, 1990

Name _____

_____ *will attend*

_____ *will not attend*

Maps and Travel Information

When the wedding couple are expecting many out-of-town guests, it is helpful to enclose a small map with the invitations. The map could include the easiest route to the church or synagogue and the reception from all directions.

For those guests who will be coming by air, train, or bus, it is also nice to include a schedule of arrivals and departures that would be appropriate for the hours of the wedding and reception. Include information about distance from the airport or train or bus station to the church or synagogue.

6

The Rehearsal Dinner or Party

G ordon's parents had divorced after Gordon and his sister had left home for college. Gordon's father had remarried, and from all appearances, his mother was getting on with her life as well.

Now, Gordon was getting married and he wanted both parents involved in the wedding. He wanted his father to be his best man. He also wanted his mother to feel special at the rehearsal dinner and wedding.

"What I'd like to do is help you plan the rehearsal dinner and pay for half of it," Gordon's mother told him. Gordon thanked his mother, told her he thought her offer was generous, and agreed to handle the arrangements with his father.

Gordon, however, only casually mentioned the rehearsal dinner to his father. When the invitation came with his mother's and father's name on them, his father merely thought his ex-wife was being "nice" to include his name on the invitations.

The night of the rehearsal went well enough. Gordon's father and stepmother were seated on one side of the room with people they knew, and his mother and sister were with mutual friends on the opposite side of the room. Gordon was pleased that his parents—although they never really spoke during the evening—*appeared* to be on friendly terms, and engaged the wedding guests in lively conversation.

When the bills came, Gordon's mother made copies, and sent them to his father with a note asking that he pay half of the cost.

A few nights later, Gordon called. "This is a real mess, Mom," he said. "Dad says he doesn't remember me ever asking him to share in the cost, and he says he's not going to pay. He says you planned the rehearsal dinner and it was your party. I'm caught in the middle."

"It's over and done with," Gordon's mother said graciously. "I'll pay for everything. There's no sense getting worked up over this."

Gordon felt terrible. He should have planned a more structured meeting with his father, shown him the estimated costs on paper, and explained to him his financial responsibility. It wasn't the end of the world, he knew, but he hated for his mother to think the worst of his father when, actually, his father had felt uninformed and left out. Gordon had handled things badly, and now his mother would have to pay for his mistake.

Planning the Rehearsal Dinner or Party

The wedding rehearsal is usually followed by a dinner or party, given by the groom's parents. If the groom's parents are divorced, consideration must be given to who will be hosting the dinner, how the invitation will be worded, the seating arrangements, etc., all of which will be covered later in this chapter.

The rehearsal dinner can be informal, such as a stand-up buffet in someone's home, or an outdoor oyster roast. Or it can be an elaborate black-tie dinner at a club or restaurant. The host or hostess decides the number of guests to be included, but all members of the wedding party and their spouses and the immediate family of the bride and groom should be included. It is also courteous to include the ceremony officiant and his or her spouse, and any out-of-town guests who are already in town for the wedding. Other guests may be included as space and budget allow.

The rehearsal dinner is the groom's parents' "big party," and when they are divorced, planning a "big party" can be stressful. The groom, with his parents, must decide who is actually going to host the dinner or party, what type of dinner or party it will be, where it will be held, and how many guests will be included.

If neither parent has remarried and they are friendly, they may choose to host the dinner together. Or, if the groom's parents are divorced and one or both are remarried, his mother and father may choose to host the rehearsal dinner together, with their spouses attending as guests.

If the groom's father and stepmother are hosting the rehearsal dinner, the groom's mother and stepfather should be invited guests and be seated at the head table or at one of the tables of honor.

If the groom's mother and stepfather are hosting the event, the groom's father and stepmother are invited and seated at a place of honor.

If the groom's father has remarried and the groom is close to his mother and his stepmother, the three may choose to host the dinner together.

If both parents are remarried, both couples may choose to host the dinner together. This means the stepparents will be hosting the dinner also, and their names will be included on the invitation.

In some cases, the divorce has been very bitter and a stepparent may be "controversial." In this case, he or she may tactfully choose not to attend.

The question of whether or not to invite stepfamilies to the rehearsal dinner is a delicate one. Unless the stepfamilies (stepbrothers, stepsisters, and/or stepgrandparents) are close to the bride and groom, they should not be included.

Sometimes the groom may find that relations are so strained between his parents that he may choose to host the rehearsal dinner himself, or with his bride. The rehearsal dinner could also be given by a close friend or relative, or by the bride's family.

Wording the Invitation

Before you can decide how to word the invitation to the rehearsal dinner or party, a decision must be made as to who will be the host. The parent (or parents) who is paying for the dinner generally acts as host and issues the invitation. Traditionally, the groom's parents pay for the rehearsal dinner and act as hosts. However, when the groom's parents are divorced, this may not be the case. The groom and his parents must decide who is going to pay for the dinner, and therefore issue the invitation.

If one or both of the groom's parents are hosting the rehearsal dinner or party, there are many different ways to word the invitation. Everyone's situation is different. The examples in this chapter illustrate some of the more common situations that may occur.

Rehearsal Dinner or Party Invitation Examples

For each of the following situations, we have provided a formal and an informal invitation. Look through the list below to select the situation that best applies to your particular case.

1. *Neither of groom's parents remarried; hosting together*

2. *Groom's mother and/or father remarried; only groom's mother and father hosting*

3. *Groom's father and stepmother hosting*

4. *Groom's mother and stepfather hosting*

5. *Only groom's father remarried; groom's mother, father, and stepmother hosting*

6. *Only groom's mother remarried; groom's mother, stepfather, and father hosting*

7. *Both groom's parents remarried; all four hosting together*

8. *Groom (or bride and groom) hosting*

1. Neither of groom's parents remarried; hosting together

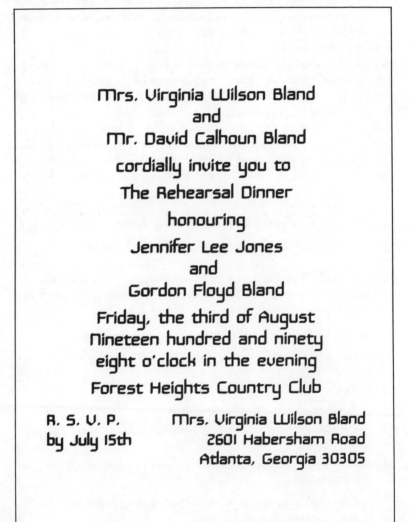

Mrs. Virginia Wilson Bland
and
Mr. David Calhoun Bland
cordially invite you to
The Rehearsal Dinner
honouring
Jennifer Lee Jones
and
Gordon Floyd Bland
Friday, the third of August
Nineteen hundred and ninety
eight o'clock in the evening
Forest Heights Country Club

R. S. V. P.   Mrs. Virginia Wilson Bland
by July 15th   2601 Habersham Road
                                  Atlanta, Georgia 30305

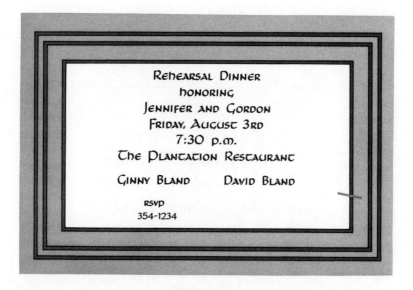

Rehearsal Dinner
honoring
Jennifer and Gordon
Friday, August 3rd
7:30 p.m.
The Plantation Restaurant

Ginny Bland   David Bland

RSVP
354-1234

Responses are usually made to the groom's mother, but this is a decision to be made by those hosting the party.

2. *Groom's mother and/or father remarried; only groom's mother and father hosting*

Stepparents attend as guests.

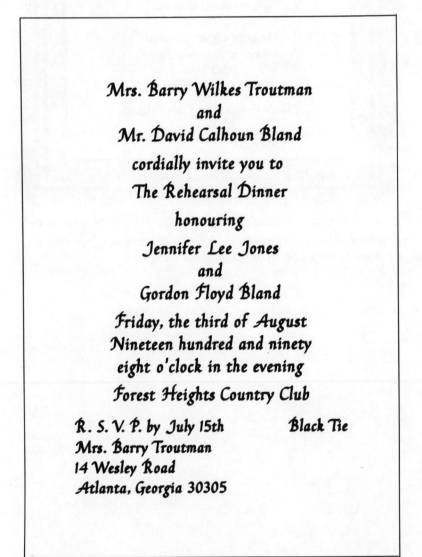

Mrs. Barry Wilkes Troutman
and
Mr. David Calhoun Bland

cordially invite you to

The Rehearsal Dinner

honouring

Jennifer Lee Jones
and
Gordon Floyd Bland

Friday, the third of August
Nineteen hundred and ninety
eight o'clock in the evening

Forest Heights Country Club

R. S. V. P. by July 15th   Black Tie
Mrs. Barry Troutman
14 Wesley Road
Atlanta, Georgia 30305

Responses are usually made to the groom's mother, but this is a decision to be made by those hosting the party.

3. Groom's father and stepmother hosting

Mr. and Mrs. David Bland
cordially invite you to
The Rehearsal Dinner
honoring
Jennifer and Gordon
Friday, the third of August
seven-thirty in the evening
Forrest Heights Country Club
R.S.V.P.
912-354-1234

Rehearsal Party
Shrimp Boil
honoring
Jennifer and Gordon
Friday, August 3rd
7:30 p.m.
The Yacht Club
43 Navigator Road
Judy and David Bland
R.S.V.P.
912-354-1234

4. Groom's mother and stepfather hosting

Rehearsal Dinner
honoring
Jennifer Lee Jones
and
Gordon Floyd Bland
Friday, the third of August
eight o'clock in the evening
Forest City Country Club
Mr. and Mrs. Barry Wilkes Troutman

R.S.V.P.   14 Wesley Road
by July 15   Atlanta, Georgia 30305

Please join us
at the Rehearsal Dinner
in honor of
Jennifer Jones and Gordon Bland
Friday, August 3rd
7:30 p.m.
The Plantation Restaurant
Ginny and Barry Troutman

R.S.V.P.
912-354-1234

5. Only groom's father remarried; groom's mother, father, and stepmother hosting

Groom's mother's name appears first.

MRS. VIRGINIA WILSON BLAND
AND
MR. AND MRS. DAVID CALHOUN BLAND
CORDIALLY INVITE YOU TO
THE REHEARSAL DINNER
HONOURING
JENNIFER LEE JONES
AND
GORDON FLOYD BLAND
FRIDAY, THE THIRD OF AUGUST
NINETEEN HUNDRED AND NINETY
SEVEN-THIRTY IN THE EVENING
FOREST HEIGHTS COUNTRY CLUB

R.S.V.P. BY
JULY FIFTEENTH

MRS. VIRGINIA BLAND
2601 HABERSHAM ROAD
ATLANTA, GEORGIA 30305

REHEARSAL PARTY
HONORING
JENNIFER AND GORDON
FRIDAY, AUGUST 3RD
7:30 P.M.
THE PLANTATION RESTAURANT
GINNY BLAND *   JUDY AND DAVID BLAND

* RSVP
354-1234

Responses are usually made to the groom's mother, but this is a decision to be made by those hosting the party.

6. *Only groom's mother remarried; groom's mother, stepfather, and father hosting*

Groom's mother's and stepfather's names appear first.

Mr. and Mrs. Barry Wilkes Troutman
and
Mr. David Calhoun Bland
cordially invite you to
The Rehearsal Dinner
honouring
Jennifer Lee Jones
and
Gordon Floyd Bland
Friday, the third of August
Nineteen hundred and ninety
seven-thirty in the evening
Forest Heights Country Club

Rsvp by
July fifteenth

Mrs. Barry Troutman
14 Wesley Road
Atlanta, Georgia 30305

Rehearsal Party
honoring
Jennifer and Gordon

Friday, August 3rd
7:30 p.m.

The Plantation Restaurant

Ginny and Barry Troutman   David Bland

RSVP
354-1234

Responses are usually made to the groom's mother, but this is a decision to be made by those hosting the party.

7. Both of groom's parents remarried; all four hosting together
Groom's mother's and stepfather's names appear first.

Mr. and Mrs. Barry Wikes Troutman
and
Mr. and Mrs. David Calhoun Bland
cordially invite you to
The Rehearsal Dinner
honouring
Jennifer Lee Jones and Gordon Floyd Bland
Friday, the third of August
Nineteen hundred and ninety
Eight o'clock in the evening
Forest Heights Country Club

Respond please   Cocktail Attire
by July 15th
Mrs. Barry Troutman
14 Wesley Road
Atlanta, Georgia 30605

REHEARSAL DINNER
HONORING
JENNIFER AND GORDON

FRIDAY, AUGUST 3RD   7:30 P.M.
THE PLANTATION RESTAURANT

GINNY AND BARRY TROUTMAN   JUDY AND DAVID BLAND

RSVP
354-1234

Responses are usually made to the groom's mother, but this is a decision to be made by those hosting the party.

8. Groom (or bride and groom) hosting

Rehearsal Dinner
honoring
Jennifer and Gordon
Friday, August 3rd
7:30 p. m.
Forest Heights Country Club
R. S. V. P.
354-1234

Please Join Us
at
Our Rehearsal Dinner
Friday, August 3rd
8:00 p. m.
Forest Heights Country Club
Jennifer Lee Jones   Gordon Floyd Bland
R. S. V. P. by July 15th
355-1234

Preprinted Invitations

Most card shops and stationers have preprinted rehearsal dinner or party invitations from which to choose. These are perfectly acceptable, and certainly less expensive than custom-printed cards.

Seating Arrangements

Planning the seating arrangement at the rehearsal dinner or party when parents are divorced is no simple matter. Thinking through the seating and preparing ahead are essential. The hostess may find it helpful to sit down and draw out her tables before trying to arrange the place cards, which are a necessity.

The bride and groom should always be seated together at the rehearsal dinner or party. A head table is not necessary, especially if your parents are divorced. Round tables, separating everyone, may be the best plan, because this allows there to be more than one table of honor. Tables of honor would include the bride and groom's table, the groom's mother's table, the groom's father's table, and the brides' parents' table (if they are not divorced). The bride and groom may choose to seat some of their attendants at their table. The groom's mother's table should include her family and/or close friends. The groom's father's table should include his family and/or close friends. The same applies to the bride's parents' table, or tables if they are divorced. As stated earlier in this chapter, stepfamilies (stepbrothers, stepsisters, and/or stepgrandparents) should not be included in the rehearsal dinner unless they are close to the bride and groom.

On the pages following are some suggested seating arrangements for the rehearsal dinner or party.

Rehearsal Dinner or Party Seating Arrangement Examples

The following seating examples illustrate different ways to seat your guests according to your particular situation.

1. *Groom's parents divorced; mother remarried; with head table*
2. *Groom's parents divorced; father remarried; with head table*
3. *Groom's parents divorced; mother or father remarried; no head table*
4. *Groom's parents divorced; both remarried; large head table*
5. *Groom's parents divorced; both remarried; small head table*
6. *Groom's parents divorced; both remarried; no head table*
7. *Bride's parents and groom's parents divorced; all remarried; with head table*
8. *Bride's parents and groom's parents divorced; all remarried; no head table; large seated dinner*
9. *Bride's parents and groom's parents divorced; all remarried; no head table; small seated dinner*
10. *Bride's parents divorced; mother remarried; with head table*
11. *Bride's parents divorced; father remarried; with head table*
12. *Bride's parents divorced; mother or father remarried; no head table*
13. *Bride's parents divorced; both remarried; large head table*
14. *Bride's parents divorced; both remarried; small head table*
15. *Bride's parents divorced; both remarried; no head table*

1. Groom's parents divorced; mother remarried; with head table

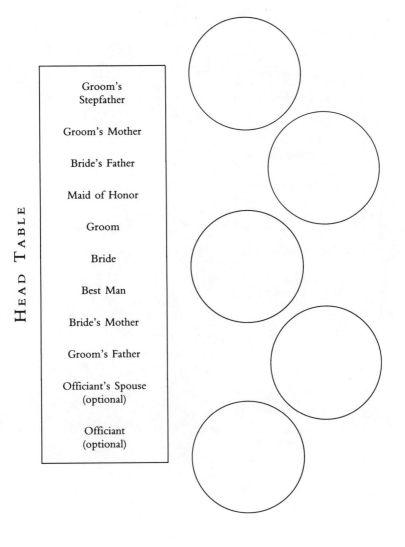

HEAD TABLE

Groom's
Stepfather

Groom's Mother

Bride's Father

Maid of Honor

Groom

Bride

Best Man

Bride's Mother

Groom's Father

Officiant's Spouse
(optional)

Officiant
(optional)

2. *Groom's parents divorced; father remarried; with head table*

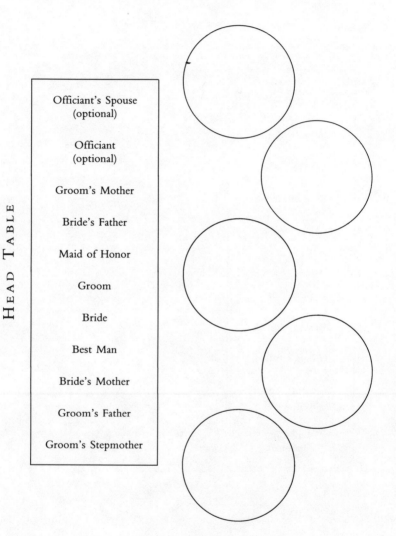

HEAD TABLE

Officiant's Spouse
(optional)

Officiant
(optional)

Groom's Mother

Bride's Father

Maid of Honor

Groom

Bride

Best Man

Bride's Mother

Groom's Father

Groom's Stepmother

3. Groom's parents divorced; mother or father remarried; no head table

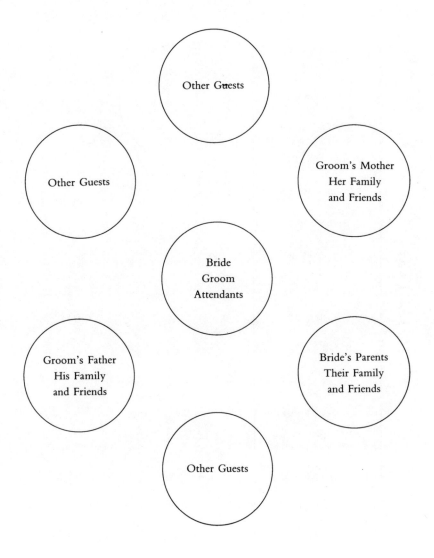

4. *Groom's parents divorced; both remarried; large head table*

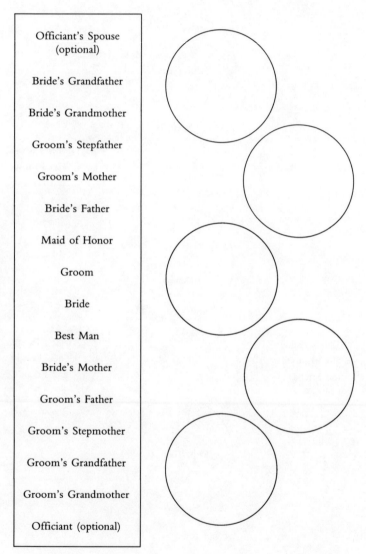

HEAD TABLE

Officiant's Spouse (optional)

Bride's Grandfather

Bride's Grandmother

Groom's Stepfather

Groom's Mother

Bride's Father

Maid of Honor

Groom

Bride

Best Man

Bride's Mother

Groom's Father

Groom's Stepmother

Groom's Grandfather

Groom's Grandmother

Officiant (optional)

5. Groom's parents divorced; both remarried; small head table

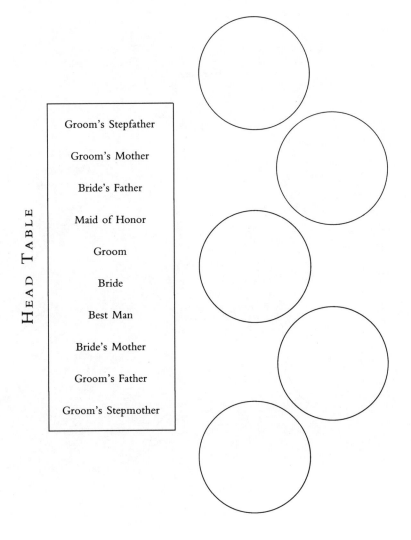

HEAD TABLE

Groom's Stepfather

Groom's Mother

Bride's Father

Maid of Honor

Groom

Bride

Best Man

Bride's Mother

Groom's Father

Groom's Stepmother

6. Groom's parents divorced; both remarried; no head table

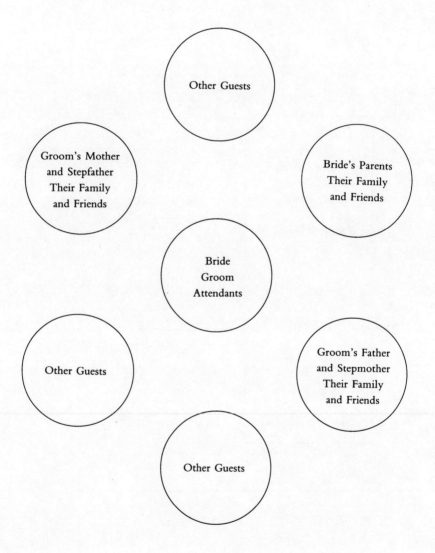

7. *Bride's parents and groom's parents divorced; all remarried; with head table*

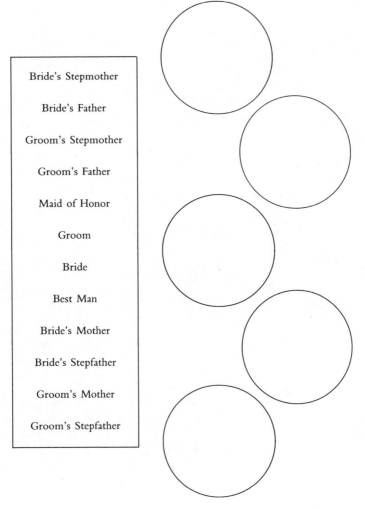

HEAD TABLE

Bride's Stepmother

Bride's Father

Groom's Stepmother

Groom's Father

Maid of Honor

Groom

Bride

Best Man

Bride's Mother

Bride's Stepfather

Groom's Mother

Groom's Stepfather

8. *Bride's parents and groom's parents divorced; all remarried; no head table; large seated dinner*

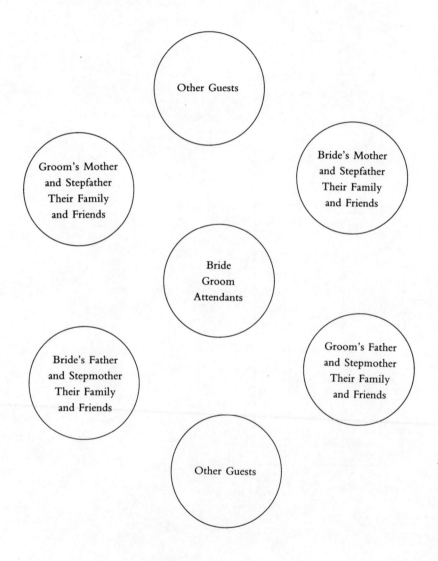

9. *Bride's parents and groom's parents divorced; all remarried; no head table; small seated dinner*

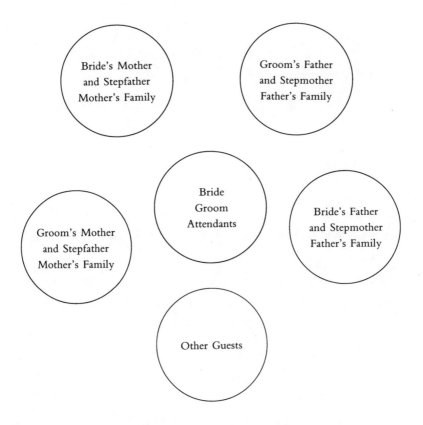

10. Bride's parents divorced; mother remarried; with head table

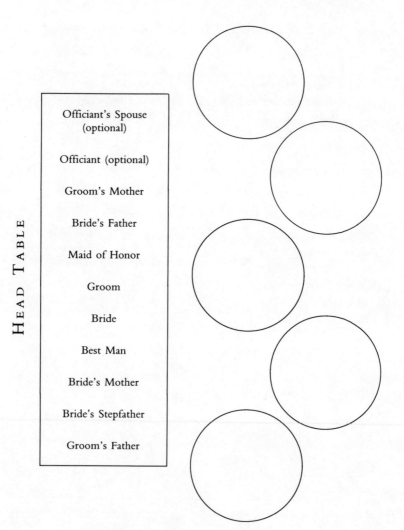

HEAD TABLE

Officiant's Spouse (optional)

Officiant (optional)

Groom's Mother

Bride's Father

Maid of Honor

Groom

Bride

Best Man

Bride's Mother

Bride's Stepfather

Groom's Father

11. Bride's parents divorced; father remarried; with head table

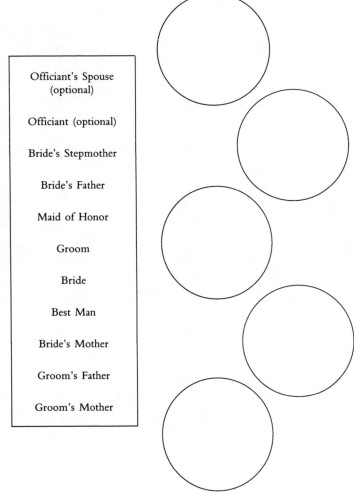

HEAD TABLE

Officiant's Spouse
(optional)

Officiant (optional)

Bride's Stepmother

Bride's Father

Maid of Honor

Groom

Bride

Best Man

Bride's Mother

Groom's Father

Groom's Mother

12. Bride's parents divorced; mother or father remarried; no head table

13. *Bride's parents divorced; both remarried; large head table*

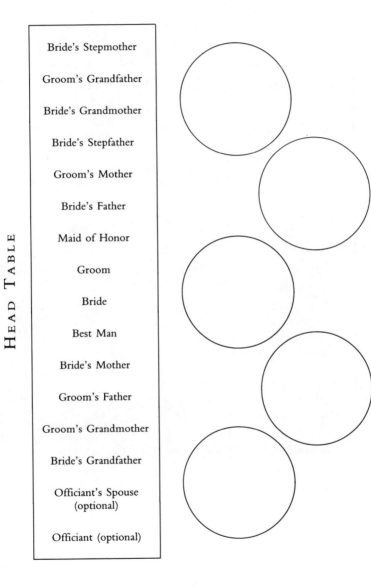

HEAD TABLE

Bride's Stepmother

Groom's Grandfather

Bride's Grandmother

Bride's Stepfather

Groom's Mother

Bride's Father

Maid of Honor

Groom

Bride

Best Man

Bride's Mother

Groom's Father

Groom's Grandmother

Bride's Grandfather

Officiant's Spouse
(optional)

Officiant (optional)

14. *Bride's parents divorced; both remarried; small head table*

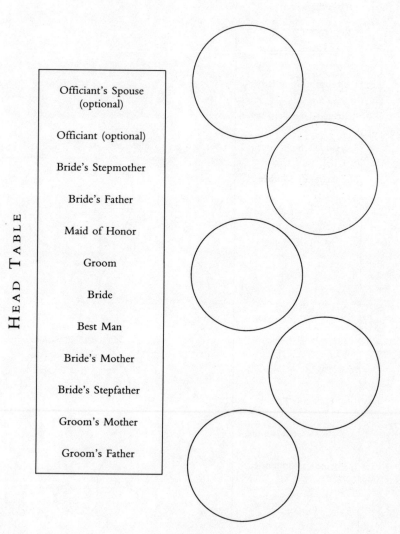

HEAD TABLE

Officiant's Spouse
(optional)

Officiant (optional)

Bride's Stepmother

Bride's Father

Maid of Honor

Groom

Bride

Best Man

Bride's Mother

Bride's Stepfather

Groom's Mother

Groom's Father

15. Bride's parents divorced; both remarried; no head table

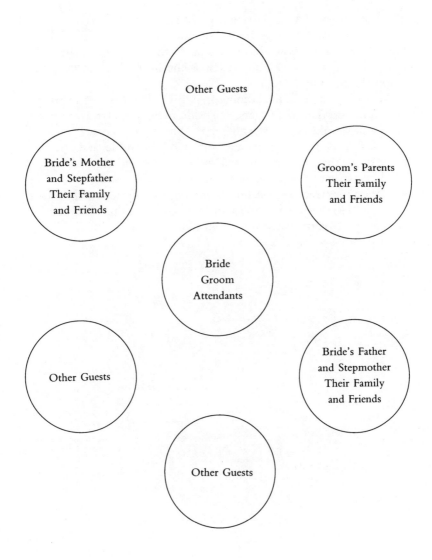

Toasting

The host, who may be the groom's father or stepfather, can begin the toasting, welcoming the guests and saying something about how happy he is about the marriage. In the cases when someone other than the father or stepfather is the host, the best man can begin the toasting.

Anyone at the rehearsal dinner may propose a toast—the bride's father, her mother, the ushers, the bridesmaids, and family friends.

Toasts should be short and sweet. Some may be sentimental, others funny, focusing on the antics of the bride and groom. Sometimes the bridesmaids will make up a poem to read.

The host may also want to signal an end to the festivities—after all, everyone needs to rest up for the big day ahead—with a toast such as: "I know Jennifer and Gordon join me in thanking you for being a part of this special time in their lives. Good night."

7

The Wedding Ceremony

The groom's father and stepmother did not attend the rehearsal. The next day, at the wedding, they did not come back to the bride's room before the ceremony, as expected.

Everyone waited. And waited.

The wedding director anxiously approached the groom. "Where are your father and stepmother?" she asked.

"I *know* they're coming," he said, nervously.

But it was time for the ceremony, and the director began to gather the wedding party at the back of the church to prepare for the processional.

She seated the bride's grandmother. The groom's father and stepmother were to be seated next.

She glanced at the door. She glanced at her watch. It was just minutes before the hour, and she would have to continue.

She seated the groom's mother, then the bride's mother. The soloist began. The wedding had started. A couple appeared at the door.

"If you will wait just a minute, you can go up to the balcony and find a seat," the director said politely. "We have already seated the bride's mother, and no one else should be formally seated now," she whispered in explanation.

A member of the wedding party leaned over. "Do you know that's the groom's father and stepmother?" All the planning in the world had not prepared the wedding director for this situation.

The director found the bride, leaned in close so that no one else could hear, and asked, "What do you want me to do?"

The bride, poised to go down the aisle, said just one word, "Nothing."

The wedding director took her cue, and quietly spoke to the father and stepmother. "If you'd like, you can slip in the church and find a seat in the back," she suggested. "Fine," said the father in a hushed voice.

Just as they sat down, the groom's brother jumped from his seat in the church and rushed back to the vestibule. "Who's running this show?" he demanded.

"I am," the wedding director said.

"Do you realize you just seated the father of the groom in the back of the church?" he said in an angry whisper.

"They were late. The mothers were already seated, and I asked them to find their own seats," she said. "Now, if you will excuse me, I have a wedding to direct."

Following the ceremony, the director found the groom, told him what she'd done, and took full responsibility for her decision. She didn't mention that the bride had helped her make it.

"You did the right thing" was the groom's surprising response. "My father and stepmother did the same thing at my brother's wedding. She wanted to be the last mother seated, and this was her way of making sure she would be."

"I should have been warned," said the director later. "This illustrates the need to plan ahead. Sometimes on-the-spot decisions have to be made, and everyone has to remember that it is the bride and groom's wedding, above everything else."

Planning the Ceremony

It would be impossible to try to give examples for all the complicated situations that can arise when dealing with divorces and stepfamilies. It is the intent of this chapter to illustrate the most common situations, in the hope that the bride will be able to use them as guidelines in making her own wedding plans.

If the bride foresees uncomfortable and complicated situations, she should try to engage a competent, experienced wedding director who has been faced with these situations before, and can help work out solutions to her particular problems.

The Wedding Rehearsal

A rehearsal, usually the night before the wedding ceremony, needs to be just that—a rehearsal of what will take place the next day. The clergy or officiant and the director or whoever is helping should be present. It is also helpful for the musicians to attend. The ceremony will be just as the bride and groom dreamed, *if* there is a successful rehearsal.

The rehearsal is especially important when the bride's or groom's parents are divorced. Details should be worked out ahead of the rehearsal so that everyone feels comfortable with the decisions concerning the seating arrangements for the parents, ushering procedures, and altar procedures.

The seating in a divorced situation can be awkward and confusing. The bride may not be able to abide by established rules of etiquette, and instead she may determine the seating based on common sense and sensitivity for the feelings of both families. The ushers should be made aware of each delicate situation at the rehearsal by the director or whoever is helping. (See seating suggestions throughout this chapter.)

Rehearsal Suggestions

• All members of the wedding party should be at the rehearsal, along with the officiant, musicians, and wedding director.

• Decide before the rehearsal if the bride is going to participate in the rehearsal or have someone stand in for her. (Most brides today choose to rehearse themselves.)

- If the bride has two honor attendants (maid and matron of honor), she must decide who will hold her bouquet and the groom's ring during the ceremony.

- Decide which of the bride's father's arms she will hold when she walks down the aisle. This should be discussed with the officiant.

- Decide who will lift the bride's veil at the altar. This may be done by her honor attendant, the groom, or her father.

- The director or whoever is helping will instruct the ushers as to their duties. (See "Ushers' Duties," pages 158–159, and "Formal Ushering and Seating," below.)

- Rehearse the formal seating with the ushers. Decide at this point which usher will seat the mothers, stepmothers, grandmothers, and any other honored guests.

- Remind the wedding party of any last-minute details: the time to be at the church or synagogue, photography schedule, etc.

Formal Ushering and Seating

SEATING THE MOTHERS, STEPMOTHERS, AND GRANDMOTHERS

The ushering of family members—those who will be formally seated—should begin about ten minutes before the wedding. This time will vary according to the number of guests to be formally seated. The ultimate goal is to seat the bride's mother immediately prior to the ceremony.

Those who will be formally seated should be decided upon by the bride and groom before the rehearsal, and this information should be discussed with the director, or whoever is conducting the rehearsal.

Individual circumstances determine the seating of the parents. These arrangements should be decided before the rehearsal so that everyone is comfortable and prepared. Work out these details with the director, and let her or him place everyone. An outsider, not emotionally involved, is the best person to handle this sometimes sticky job. If the bride has no director, try to find someone other than a family member who can help carry out the seating plans. Use this chapter to help decide exactly where everyone should sit.

The bride's mother and the groom's mother are seated in the first pews, unless the bride or groom has had little or no contact with her or his mother and chooses to have her or his stepmother sit in the front pew. In a Jewish ceremony, the parents sometimes escort the bride and groom to the altar, and therefore are not seated.

In formally seating the bride's grandmothers, stepmother, and mother, the designated usher offers his right arm and walks each down the aisle to her special seat on the left side of the church or synagogue. (In an Orthodox or a Conservative Jewish ceremony, the bride's family sits on the right side of the synagogue.) He stops at her designated pew and she crosses in front of him to be seated. After she is seated, he turns and returns up the aisle to the vestibule. When the groom's grandmothers, stepmother, and mother are to be seated, the designated usher offers his right arm and ushers each to her special seat on the right side of the church or synagogue. After she is seated, he returns to the vestibule.

When ushering the bride's mother, stepmother, and grandmothers out of the ceremony, the designated usher walks down the aisle, turns, and stands beside the pew of the lady he is escorting out. He extends her a hand to help her from her seat, and then offers her his right arm to escort her up the aisle. When the groom's mother, stepmother, or grandmother is to be ushered out, the designated usher walks down the aisle to the pew where she is sitting. He turns to face the congregation and offers his left hand to help the honored guest from her seat. She then crosses in front of him to take his right arm and is escorted up the aisle.

Under normal circumstances, the order in which the family is ushered in is reversed for ushering out. In other words, the bride's mother is ushered in last, and ushered out first. This order, however, can—and often does—change when stepparents are involved.

Fill in the chart and lists on pages 147–149 to determine the special seating arrangement before the rehearsal. (Use a pencil so changes can easily be made.) Discuss this at one of the meetings with the director prior to the rehearsal, as it will be her or his responsibility to direct the ushering and seating.

Choose from the example below the one that best suits your situation to help determine the order for ushering and the seating arrangement. Each example is discussed later in this chapter.

Bride's Parents Divorced

1. *Neither remarried and parents friendly*
2. *Bride not close to stepmother*
3. *Bride close to stepmother*
4. *Bride's father not remarried; mother may or may not be remarried; parents not friendly*
5. *Controversial stepparent*

Groom's Parents Divorced

1. *Neither remarried and parents friendly*
2. *Groom's father and/or mother remarried; father not acting as best man*
3. *Groom's father remarried and acting as best man; groom not close to stepmother; mother remarried or not*
4. *Groom's father remarried and acting as best man; groom close to stepmother; mother remarried or not*
5. *Groom's father not remarried; mother may or may not be remarried; parents not friendly*

Other Circumstances

1. *Bride's and groom's parents divorced and all remarried*
2. *Bride or groom raised by father and stepmother and had little or no contact with mother*
3. *Longtime companions*

Bride's Parents Divorced

1. *Neither remarried and parents friendly*

   a. Order for ushering in
   Groom's grandparents
   Bride's grandparents
   Groom's mother and father
   Bride's mother

   b. Order for ushering out
   Bride's mother and father. He may follow behind the bride's
   mother when she is formally ushered out. This may be
   done whether he is sitting with her or not.
   Groom's mother and father
   Bride's grandparents
   Groom's grandparents

   c. First suggested seating arrangement
   First pew: Bride's mother (may have her parents or other
   close relative join her)
   Second pew: Bride's mother's family, i.e., grandparents,
   aunts, uncles, etc. If there are too many relatives for this
   pew, the bride may choose to have her maternal grandparents sit in the first pew with her mother.
   Third pew: Bride's father (after escorting the bride down the
   aisle and giving her away) sits in this pew with his family.

   d. Second suggested seating arrangement
   First pew: Bride's mother with her parents or other close
   relative if she chooses not to sit alone
   Second pew: Bride's father may sit immediately behind his
   ex-wife if the bride's mother has no other family for this
   pew and the bride's parents are friendly. He may have his
   parents or other close relatives join him in this pew.

  e. Third suggested seating arrangement
  First pew: Bride's mother and father. (This is acceptable if
  the bride's parents are friendly and choose to sit together.)
  Second pew: Bride's maternal grandparents, aunts, uncles,
  etc.
  Third pew: Bride's paternal grandparents, aunts, uncles, etc.

If none of the previous seating arrangements are acceptable, the
bride and her director should work out an arrangement with her
parents that is acceptable to everyone.

2. *Bride not close to stepmother*

  a. Order for ushering in
  Bride's stepmother. (If she is controversial, see the ushering
  and seating suggestions on page 137.)
  Groom's grandparents
  Bride's grandparents
  Groom's mother and father
  Bride's mother, or mother and stepfather

  b. Order for ushering out
  Bride's mother, or mother and stepfather
  Groom's mother and father
  Bride's father and stepmother
  Bride's grandparents
  Groom's grandparents

  c. Suggested seating arrangement
  First pew: Bride's mother and stepfather, if she has remarried
  Second pew: Bride's mother's family, i.e., grandparents,
  aunts, uncles, etc. If there are too many relatives for this
  pew, the bride may choose to have her maternal grandparents sit in the first pew with her mother.
  Third pew: Bride's father (after escorting the bride down the
  aisle and giving her away) sits with his wife, if he has
  remarried, and their family.

3. *Bride close to stepmother*

   a. Order for ushering in
        Groom's grandparents
        Bride's grandparents
        Bride's stepmother
        Groom's mother and father (if he is not acting as best man)
        Bride's mother, or mother and stepfather

   b. Order for ushering out
        Bride's mother, or mother and stepfather
        Groom's mother and father
        Bride's father and stepmother
        Bride's grandparents
        Groom's grandparents

   c. First suggested seating arrangement
        First pew: Bride's mother and stepfather, if she has remarried
        Second pew: Bride's mother's family, i.e., grandparents, aunts, uncles, etc. If there are too many relatives for this pew, the bride may choose to have her maternal grandparents sit in the first pew with her mother.
        Third pew: Bride's father (after escorting the bride down the aisle and giving her away) sits with his wife, if he has remarried, and their family.

   d. Second suggested seating arrangement (Bride's parents are friendly and/or the bride's father is paying for the wedding.)
        First pew: Bride's mother and stepfather, if she has remarried
        Second pew: Bride's father and stepmother, if he has remarried. He may sit immediately behind his ex-wife if the bride's mother has no other family for this pew and the bride's parents are friendly. He may choose to have his parents or other close relatives to join him in this pew.

There are times when the bride's father assumes *all* of the wedding expenses and prefers to sit in the second rather than the third pew. His wishes should be considered. If parents and stepparents are friendly, they may sit in the first pew together.

4. *Bride's father not remarried; mother may or may not be remarried; parents not friendly*

   a. Order for ushering in
   Groom's grandparents
   Bride's grandparents
   Groom's mother and father (if he is not acting as best man)
   Bride's mother, or mother and stepfather

   b. Order for ushering out
   Bride's mother, or mother and stepfather
   Groom's mother and father
   Bride's father. It is important for the bride's father to formally exit the ceremony. When he has not remarried, a decision must be made as to how he will exit. If his parents are being ushered out, he may follow behind them. Another suggestion would be for his daughter, a sister, or another close female relative to sit with him. She could then be formally ushered out, and he could follow. She should not be formally ushered in. He could also choose to exit alone after the groom's parents have been formally ushered out.
   Bride's grandparents
   Groom's grandparents

   c. Suggested seating arrangement
   First pew: Bride's mother, or mother and stepfather
   Second pew: Bride's mother's family, i.e., grandparents, aunts, uncles, etc. If there are too many relatives for this pew, the bride may choose to have her maternal grandparents sit in the first pew with her mother.
   Third pew: Bride's father (after escorting the bride down the aisle and giving her away) sits in this pew with his family.

5. *Controversial stepparent*

   a. Ushering
   - If, after a great deal of consideration and discussion, the bride's stepmother is to be seated in the reserved pews with her husband but not formally ushered in, then she should be escorted to her seat when she arrives at the ceremony, preferably fifteen minutes early. The bride's father joins her after he gives his daughter away. If his wife is not going to be formally ushered out of the ceremony, she and the bride's father may exit the ceremony together after the groom's mother is formally ushered out. Be sure this is practiced at the rehearsal.

   - If the bride's stepfather is controversial and he is going to sit with the bride's mother in the reserved pews, he should arrive at the ceremony early and take his seat in the front pew. He may or may not follow his wife when she is formally ushered out of the ceremony. This should be decided before the rehearsal.

   b. Seating
   - Seating a "controversial" stepparent at the wedding ceremony is probably one of the most delicate dilemmas to occur when parents are divorced. This situation occurs when the divorce has caused great bitterness. It requires the utmost consideration and understanding on everyone's part and should definitely be arranged before the rehearsal. Again, a competent director can help, not only with the decision on where the stepparent will sit, but also in dealing with all parents when discussing the seating. The bride and groom should keep in mind that this is not a casual companion, but a parent's spouse. If the bride's or groom's controversial stepparent is going to attend the wedding, then he or she should be seated with his or her spouse.

   - If no compromise can be reached and tensions are high, the controversial stepparent—as an act of goodwill toward the wedding couple—may elect not to attend the wedding.

c. Suggested seating arrangement

First pew: Bride's mother, or mother and stepfather (may have her parents or other close relative join her)

Second pew: Bride's mother's family, i.e., grandparents, aunts, uncles, etc. If there are too many relatives for this pew, the bride may choose to have her maternal grandparents sit in the first pew with her mother.

Third pew: Bride's father (after escorting the bride down the aisle and giving her away) sits in this pew with his wife and his family.

Groom's Parents Divorced

1. *Neither remarried and parents friendly*

a. Order for ushering in

Groom's grandparents

Bride's grandparents

Groom's mother. The groom's father follows behind her.

Bride's mother

b. Order for ushering out

Bride's mother and father

Groom's mother. The groom's father may follow behind her when she is formally ushered out. This may be done whether he is sitting with her or not.

Bride's grandparents

Groom's grandparents

c. First suggested seating arrangement

First pew: Groom's mother (may have her parents or other close relatives join her)

Second pew: Groom's mother's family, i.e., grandparents, aunts, uncles, etc. If there are too many relatives for this pew, the groom may choose to have his maternal grandparents sit in the first pew with his mother.

Third pew: Groom's father sits in this pew with his family.

d. Second suggested seating arrangement

First pew: Groom's mother with her parents or other close relative if she chooses not to sit alone

Second pew: Groom's father. He may sit immediately behind his ex-wife if the groom's mother has no other family for this pew and the groom's parents are friendly. He may choose to have his parents or other close relatives join him in this pew.

e. Third suggested seating arrangement

First pew: Groom's mother and father. (This is acceptable if the groom's parents are friendly and choose to sit together.)

Second pew: Groom's maternal grandparents, aunts, uncles, etc.

Third pew: Groom's paternal grandparents, aunts, uncles, etc.

If none of these are acceptable, the groom and the director should work out an arrangement that is acceptable to everyone.

2. *Groom's father and/or mother remarried; father not acting as best man*

a. Order for ushering in
Groom's grandparents
Bride's grandparents
Groom's father and stepmother
Groom's mother, or mother and stepfather
Bride's mother

b. Order for ushering out
Bride's mother and father
Groom's mother, or mother and stepfather
Groom's father and stepmother
Bride's grandparents
Groom's grandparents

c. First suggested seating arrangement
First pew: Groom's mother, or mother and stepfather
Second pew: Groom's mother's family, i.e., grandparents, aunts, uncles, etc. If there are too many relatives for this pew, the groom may choose to have his maternal grandparents sit in the first pew with his mother.
Third pew: Groom's father and stepmother and his family

d. Second suggested seating arrangement
First pew: Groom's mother, or mother and stepfather
Second pew: Groom's father and stepmother. He may sit immediately behind his ex-wife if the groom's mother has no other family for this pew and the groom's parents are friendly. He may choose to have his parents or other close relatives join him in this pew.

If neither of these is acceptable, the groom and the director should work out an arrangement that is acceptable to everyone.

3. *Groom's father remarried and acting as best man; groom not close to stepmother; mother remarried or not*

a. Order for ushering in
Groom's stepmother. If the groom's stepmother is controversial and the groom's father is acting as best man, then the groom may choose to have his stepmother *not* sit with the family. She should be escorted to a seat (not in the reserved section) when she arrives at the ceremony, preferably fifteen minutes early. She may choose not to attend the ceremony at all.
Groom's grandparents
Bride's grandparents
Groom's mother, or mother and stepfather
Bride's mother

b. Order for ushering out
Bride's mother and father
Groom's mother, or mother and stepfather
Bride's grandparents
Groom's grandparents
Groom's stepmother

c. Suggested seating arrangement
First pew: Groom's mother, or mother and stepfather
Second pew: Groom's mother's family, i.e., grandparents, aunts, uncles, etc. If there are too many relatives for this pew, the groom may choose to have his maternal grandparents sit in the first pew with his mother.
Third pew or another reserved pew: Groom's stepmother (if she is to be seated in the reserved section)

4. *Groom's father remarried and acting as best man; groom close to stepmother; mother remarried or not*

a. Order for ushering in
Groom's grandparents
Bride's grandparents
Groom's stepmother
Groom's mother, or mother and stepfather
Bride's mother

b. Order for ushering out
Bride's mother and father
Groom's mother, or mother and stepfather
Groom's stepmother
Bride's grandparents
Groom's grandparents

c. First suggested seating arrangement
First pew: Groom's mother, or mother and stepfather
Second pew: Groom's mother's family, i.e., grandparents, aunts, uncles, etc. If there are too many relatives for this pew, the groom may choose to have his maternal grandparents sit in the first pew with his mother.
Third pew: Groom's stepmother and groom's father's family

d. Second suggested seating arrangement
   If the groom's parents and stepparents are friendly, and everyone agrees, the groom's stepmother may sit in the second pew, immediately behind the groom's mother.

5. *Groom's father not remarried; mother may or may not be remarried; parents not friendly*

   a. Order for ushering in
      Groom's grandparents
      Bride's grandparents
      Groom's father. An usher could walk in with him, or he may walk in alone.
      Groom's mother, or mother and stepfather
      Bride's mother

   b. Order for ushering out
      Bride's mother and father
      Groom's mother, or mother and stepfather
      Groom's father. It is important for the groom's father to formally exit the ceremony. He may choose to exit alone, to exit with the usher who brought him in, or to follow his parents when they are formally ushered out.
      Bride's grandparents
      Groom's grandparents

   c. Suggested seating arrangement
      First pew: Groom's mother, or mother and stepfather
      Second pew: Groom's mother's family, i.e., grandparents, aunts, uncles, etc. If there are too many relatives for this pew, the groom may choose to have his maternal grandparents sit in the first pew with his mother.
      Third pew: Groom's father and his family

Other Circumstances

1. *Bride's and groom's parents divorced and all remarried*

   a. Order for ushering in
   Groom's grandparents
   Bride's grandparents
   Groom's father and stepmother
   Bride's stepmother
   Groom's mother and stepfather
   Bride's mother and stepfather

   b. Order for ushering out
   Bride's mother and stepfather
   Groom's mother and stepfather
   Bride's father and stepmother
   Groom's father and stepmother
   Bride's grandparents
   Groom's grandparents

   c. Bride's first suggested seating arrangement
   First pew: Bride's mother and stepfather.
   Second pew: Bride's mother's family, i.e., grandparents, aunts, uncles, etc. If there are too many relatives for this pew, the bride may choose to have her maternal grandparents sit in the first pew with her mother.
   Third pew: Bride's father (after escorting the bride down the aisle and giving her away) sits with his wife and his family.

   d. Bride's second suggested seating arrangement (Bride's parents are friendly and/or the bride's father is paying for the wedding.)
   First pew: Bride's mother and stepfather.
   Second pew: Bride's father and stepmother. He may sit immediately behind his ex-wife if the bride's mother has no other family for this pew and the bride's parents are friendly. He may choose to have his parents or other close relatives join him in this pew.

There are many times when the bride's father assumes *all* of the wedding expenses and prefers to sit in the second pew rather than the third pew. His wishes should be considered in the seating decisions. If parents and stepparents are friendly, and everyone agrees, they may choose to sit in the first pew together.

e. Groom's first suggested seating arrangement
First pew: Groom's mother and stepfather.
Second pew: Groom's mother's family, i.e., grandparents, aunts, uncles, etc. If there are too many relatives for this pew, the groom may choose to have his maternal grandparents sit in the first pew with his mother.
Third pew: Groom's father and stepmother and his family

f. Groom's second suggested seating arrangement
If the groom's parents and stepparents are friendly, and everyone agrees, the groom's father and stepmother may sit in the second pew immediately behind the groom's mother and stepfather, or all four may choose to sit together in the first pew.

2. *Bride or groom raised by father and stepmother and had little or no contact with mother*

a. Bride
When the bride has been raised by her father and stepmother, and has had little or no contact with her mother, she may choose that her stepmother be ushered in last (just before the processional) and ushered out first. If her biological mother chooses to attend the ceremony, she may be ushered in immediately prior to the bride's stepmother. This decision requires a great deal of discussion and thought, and should be made with everyone's feelings considered.

b. Groom

When the groom has been raised by his father and step-mother, and has had little or no contact with his mother, he may choose that his stepmother be ushered in just before the bride's mother and ushered out just after the bride's mother. If his biological mother chooses to attend the ceremony, she may be ushered in immediately prior to his stepmother. This decision requires a great deal of discussion and thought, and should be made with everyone's feelings considered.

c. Suggested seating arrangement

When the bride or groom has been brought up by the father and stepmother and has had little or no contact with the mother, the stepmother and father could sit in the first pew, with the mother in the second pew or farther back. This is a situation that would require a great deal of consideration and discussion before the rehearsal.

3. *Longtime companions*

- Traditionally, longtime companions have not been seated with the family. However, there may be times when a parent insists (especially if he or she is paying) that the companion sit with him or her during the ceremony. The bride or groom should feel comfortable with this decision.

- When the parents are divorced and not remarried it is more widely accepted for them to sit alone or with a close relative. (A casual escort is not acceptable.) If, however, the bride's or groom's father or mother insists on sitting with his or her longtime companion at the wedding, the matter should be handled with consideration and understanding from every-one. This decision should be made *before* the rehearsal. Again, a competent director or someone experienced in this area can help with both the seating decisions and dealing with the personalities involved.

- Suggested seating arrangement

  First pew: If the bride's or groom's mother has a longtime companion and insists that he sit with her, he should take his seat in the first pew when he arrives at the ceremony. He should not follow the bride's or groom's mother when she is formally ushered in or out, unless this is the bride's or groom's wish.

  Second pew: Bride's or groom's mother's family

  Third pew: Bride's or groom's father. If the bride's or groom's father has a longtime companion and insists that she sit with him, she should be ushered to her seat when she arrives at the ceremony, preferably fifteen minutes early. The bride's father joins his companion after he gives his daughter away. Companions should not be formally ushered in or out of the ceremony unless this is the bride's or groom's wish. They may exit the ceremony with the bride's or groom's father after the groom's mother is formally ushered out. Be sure this is practiced at the rehearsal.

Planning the Seating Arrangements

Fill in this chart to visualize where the honored guests will be seated. Use a pencil so changes can easily be made.

ALTAR

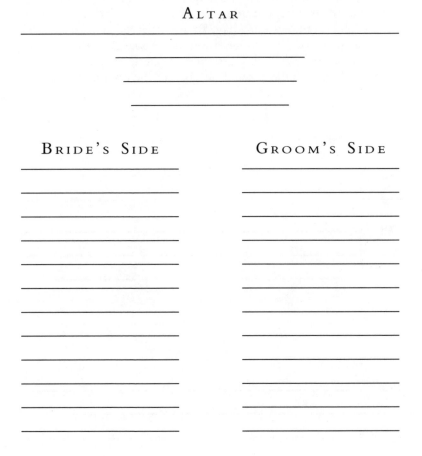

BRIDE'S SIDE   GROOM'S SIDE

Pew Assignments

Once all the seating decisions have been made, make lists for the bride's side and the groom's side. (Use pencil.) Review the lists with the director, or whoever is helping, as well as with the ushers. Give the ushers a copy during the rehearsal, and be sure to have extra copies on the wedding day. Be sure everyone understands all the arrangements. The honored guests are seated as they arrive, except for the bride's and groom's mothers, stepmothers, and grandmothers, who are seated just before the ceremony begins.

BRIDE'S SIDE

Pew 1 _____

_____

_____

Pew 2 _____

_____

_____

Pew 3 _____

_____

_____

Pew 4 _____

_____

_____

Pew 5 _____

_____

Pew 6 _____

_____

Groom's Side

Pew 1 _____

_____

_____

Pew 2 _____

_____

_____

Pew 3 _____

_____

_____

Pew 4 _____

_____

_____

Pew 5 _____

_____

Pew 6 _____

_____

An alphabetical list of all guests sitting in reserved pews should be available for the ushers in case guests forget their pew cards. (See following section, "Pew Cards.")

BRIDE'S SIDE

Name _____ Pew _____

Name _____ Pew _____

Name _____ Pew _____

Name _____ Pew _____

Name _____ Pew _____

Name _____ Pew _____

Name _____ Pew _____

Name _____ Pew _____

Name _____ Pew _____

Name _____ Pew _____

Name _____ Pew _____

Name _____ Pew _____

Name _____ Pew _____

Name _____ Pew _____

Name _____ Pew _____

Name _____ Pew _____

Name _____ Pew _____

Name _____ Pew _____

GROOM'S SIDE

Name _____ Pew _____

Name _____ Pew _____

Name _____ Pew _____

Name _____ Pew _____

Name _____ Pew _____

Name _____ Pew _____

Name _____ Pew _____

Name _____ Pew _____

Name _____ Pew _____

Name _____ Pew _____

Name _____ Pew _____

Name _____ Pew _____

Name _____ Pew _____

Name _____ Pew _____

Name _____ Pew _____

Name _____ Pew _____

Name _____ Pew _____

Name _____ Pew _____

Pew Cards

A pew card is a special card sent to those family and intimate friends who are to be seated in specially designated pews. Special pews are designated by a bouquet or white bow attached to the end of the pew. In divorce situations, pew assignments can be particularly helpful.

Pew cards can be engraved with "Pew Number ____," with the number to be filled in by hand in a style that matches the invitation. Or, for simpler weddings, the bride's mother can write the information on plain white cards or her engraved calling cards. The cards may be mailed or hand-delivered. The honored people bring the cards with them on the day of the wedding and hand them to the usher, who then knows exactly where to seat them.

The ushers are given a list of people who have been assigned special pews (see pages 150–151). This list is also helpful when guests forget to bring their pew cards. Generally, the guests identify themselves and mention to the usher that they are to sit in a reserved pew.

Pew cards should be sent to the family members and special friends the bride wishes to honor. The groom's mother should make a list, and reserved pew cards should be sent to her family and special friends also.

It is advisable to send pew cards *after* you receive acceptance to avoid empty seats or having to rework the seating plan.

For small weddings, the bride or her family can notify people by phone, and then provide the ushers with a list of names and pew assignments.

A reputable stationer can best help you with pew cards.

Altar Procedure

Here are some general guidelines for traditional altar procedures.

• Regardless of circumstances, when the clergy or officiant asks, "Who giveth this woman to be married to this man?" it is nice for the father to respond, "Her mother and I."

• In a Catholic ceremony, the bride's father is not asked this question. He turns away once he and the bride reach the altar and goes to his designated pew. In a Protestant ceremony, the bride's father usually gives the bride away. In a Reform Jewish ceremony, the bride's father does not give the bride away, but takes his seat immediately after escorting his daughter down the aisle. In an Orthodox or Conservative Jewish ceremony, the bride and groom process in with both of their parents, their fathers on their left and their mothers on their right. (See "Order for Procession and Recession," pages 154–155.) If the parents are divorced, this tradition can still be observed.

• A bride who has been brought up by her mother (who has not remarried) and who barely knew her father may choose to have a close male relative or friend of the family escort her down the aisle. At the time of giving way, he may answer, "I do," or "On behalf of her mother, I do."

• Increasingly, brides who have been brought up by their mothers alone and are very close to them ask if their mothers may escort them down the aisle. This is unconventional in a Christian ceremony, but if it is something that the bride and her mother feel good about, it certainly may be done. It is, however, traditional to have a male escort in a Christian ceremony.

• If the bride lives with her mother and stepfather and has had little or no contact with her father, the stepfather may give her away. When he does so, he should answer, "Her mother and I do."

• If the bride feels close to both her father and stepfather and she wants to include both of them in the ceremony she may choose for one of them to escort her down the aisle and the other to give her away.

- Some Jewish weddings have a chuppah, or canopy, covering the bride and groom during the service. It may be artistically designed or a simple frame covered with flowers. Many couples choose to have their parents stand under the chuppah with them during the ceremony. If the parents are divorced, this could be handled in one of the following ways:

  One solution is to eliminate the chuppah completely if the parents are uncooperative. Or simply eliminate the parents' standing under the chuppah. They would sit in their designated pews.

  If the bride and groom choose to have their parents and stepparents under the chuppah, the stepparents can be ushered in before the processional actually begins. The bride would process in with her parents and they would then join their respective spouses under the chuppah.

  If the bride's parents are not friendly and her mother objects strongly to her ex-husband's escorting the bride down the aisle, the bride may choose to walk down the aisle alone.

  Another suggestion is for the bride's stepmother to be ushered in to the chuppah, the bride's mother and stepfather to process before the bride, and the bride's father to escort his daughter down the aisle. He would then join his wife under the chuppah.

- Again, discuss all details with everyone involved before the rehearsal, so there are no surprises. A rehearsal should last only one hour. To avoid a lengthy rehearsal, all details should be worked out with the director or person helping with the wedding before the rehearsal.

Order for Procession and Recession

- A Protestant or Reform Jewish ceremony usually begins with the clergy, rabbi, or officiant entering the church or synagogue from behind the altar. He or she is followed by the groom and his best man, who take their places at the altar.

- Generally, ushers enter first, shortest to tallest. Junior bridesmaids come next, followed by the bridesmaids. The honor attendant comes next, followed by the ring bearer and finally the flowergirl. If your wedding has a simpler wedding party, the order remains the same, with the extra people eliminated. The bride comes last. She may hold either of her father's arms (consult with the officiant). The left will put her closest to the groom and make it easier for her father to slip to his pew after he has given her away.

- In a Protestant, Catholic, or Reform Jewish ceremony, when the wedding is over, the bride takes the groom's right arm and the couple starts up the aisle together. The attendants follow, beginning with the children. The honor attendant is paired with the best man, and the ushers and bridesmaids are also paired. The bridesmaids always exit on the ushers' right arm. Any extra ushers walk out together last. The ushers quickly return to escort the mothers and other honored guests.

- Jewish processions vary according to the size of the wedding, local custom, and family wishes. Ushers often enter in pairs, followed by bridesmaids in pairs or singly, followed by the groom and his best man, the honor attendant, the flowergirl, and the bride. In an Orthodox or Conservative Jewish wedding, the processional may be led by the rabbi and cantor, followed by the ushers, the bridesmaids, the best man, the groom and his parents, the bride's honor attendant or attendants, the flowergirl, and the bride and her parents, in that order. The bridesmaids may also follow the groom and his parents.

- As discussed under "Altar Procedure," this may vary when the parents are divorced. If all of the parents and stepparents are under the chuppah during the ceremony, the recession would be as follows:

> Bride and Groom
> Bride's Mother and Stepfather
> Bride's Father and Stepmother
> Groom's Parents
> Flowergirl and/or Ring Bearer
> Honor Attendants
> Bridesmaids and Ushers

Maid or Matron of Honor's Duties

A bride usually chooses her sister or best friend to be her maid or matron of honor. The maid or matron of honor's most important duties are to help the bride in the planning of her wedding, to help her during the ceremony, and to assist her in any other way needed. Her duties may include the following:

- She helps the bride address the invitations, make the favors, and run errands.

- She pays for her own wedding attire.

- She helps the bridesmaids plan a party/shower for the bride.

- She attends the wedding rehearsal and rehearsal dinner/party.

- She should arrive at the church or synagogue an hour before the ceremony, or when the bride wants her. This will depend on the photography schedule.

- She may sign the marriage license as a legal witness.

- She is expected to help the bride dress on her wedding day.

- She will hold the bride's bouquet during the ceremony, and the groom's ring if it is a double-ring ceremony.

- She assists the bride with her train at the altar.

- The bride will decide if the honor attendant or the groom will lift her veil after the wedding ceremony. The bride may choose her father to lift her veil after he gives her away.

- If the bride chooses, the maid or matron of honor may stand in the receiving line. She may also be seated in a place of honor at the reception.

Bridesmaid's Duties

- Bridesmaids help with the prewedding errands and tasks.

- Bridesmaids usually plan a party or shower for the bride.

- Bridesmaids are responsible for paying for their wedding attire and seeing that their outfit is ready on time, and that all accessories are taken care of.

- Bridesmaids attend the wedding rehearsal and the rehearsal dinner/party.

- Bridesmaids should arrive at the church or synagogue at least an hour prior to the ceremony, or when the bride wants them. This will depend on the photography schedule.

Best Man's Duties

A groom usually chooses his brother, his father, a close relative, or his best friend as his best man. The best man's duties may include the following:

- He helps the groom select wedding attire, and pays for his own.

- He attends the wedding rehearsal and the rehearsal dinner/party.

- He should arrive at the church or synagogue at least an hour before the ceremony, or whenever the groom wants him. This will depend on the photography schedule.

- He keeps the bride's wedding ring until the appropriate time during the ceremony.

- He delivers the officiant's fee on behalf of the groom.

- He may sign the marriage license as a legal witness.

- He makes the first toast to the bride and groom at the reception, if toasts are made.

- He makes sure the groom's going-away clothes are taken to the reception.

- He may take the groom's wedding attire to the cleaners or return it to the rental shop after the wedding.

Ushers' Duties

Ushers are chosen from among the groom's close friends and relatives. He often asks his brothers to usher, although he isn't obliged to do so. He frequently asks one or more of the bride's brothers to serve as well. For a large wedding, there should be plenty of ushers to seat the guests. There may be more ushers than bridesmaids. To calculate the number of ushers needed, assume that three-fourths of the invited guests will come. There should be one usher for approximately every fifty guests.

Below are some general ushers' duties. Remember—in a divorce situation, ushers should be made aware of unusual seating and ushering circumstances.

- Ushers pay for their wedding attire, and take responsibility for obtaining it. The groom has chosen the attire and the formal shop that will be used. The groom pays for the ushers' gloves and boutonnieres.

- Ushers attend the wedding rehearsal and the rehearsal dinner/party.

- On the wedding day, ushers should be at the church or synagogue at least one hour prior to the ceremony. This will depend on the photography schedule. The boutonnieres will be in the vestibule, and should be worn on the left lapel.

- Ushers group themselves in the vestibule, to the left of the door. Each of them should have a list of guests to be seated in the reserved pews.

- Ushers light the candles when asked to by the wedding director, or whoever is in charge.

- As guests arrive at the ceremony, they wait in the vestibule for an usher to seat them as soon as possible.

- Ushers should try to seat guests evenly on both sides of the church or synagogue. However, if guests indicate that they prefer the "groom's side" or the "bride's side," ushers should honor this request. The bride's family and friends are on the left side of the aisle and the groom's are on the right. This is reversed in an Orthodox or Conservative Jewish ceremony.

• The usher should extend his right arm to each female guest when ushering. If several guests arrive in a group, the usher extends his arm to the eldest lady, and walks her down the aisle to an empty seat. He then returns to make sure each of the other ladies is seated. If a female guest arrives with an escort, the usher takes her to her seat and the escort follows a few steps behind. A male guest entering alone may seat himself or be seated by the usher, who does not offer his arm unless the man is elderly and appears to be in need of assistance. Children—girls and boys under age fifteen or so—follow along behind their parents. If there is time, an usher may seat a young lady slightly under this age.

• Ushers should know who the special guests are and where they are to be seated. This is especially true in the case of divorced parents and stepparents.

• Ushers distribute the wedding programs, if there are any.

• If there is a close relative ushering, he should be asked to seat the mothers, stepmothers, and grandmothers of the bride and groom. Otherwise, any usher may assume this responsibility.

• Ushers may be assigned to roll the white aisle cloth up the center aisle in formal ceremonies. This may be done prior to the wedding, in which case guests are seated from the side aisles. If guests will be using the center aisle, the cloth is unrolled after the mother of the bride is seated, just before the beginning of the ceremony, or just before the bride enters.

• After the ushers exit in the recessional, they should quickly return to escort the mothers and other honored guests out.

8

Photography and Video

Jennifer's parents had had a rather bitter divorce—due in part to her father's extramarital affair with Judy, now his wife. Still, Jennifer was trying her best not to let her parents' divorce drastically alter the kind of wedding she wanted. She was pleasantly surprised and touched that both her mother and her father, Steve, had wanted to share equally in the wedding expenses, and wanted her to spend whatever she felt necessary to have the perfect wedding.

Things had gone smoothly enough until the morning of the wedding, when her mother seemed more apprehensive than Jennifer had expected. She realized that her mother was concerned about sharing the day with her ex-husband and his new wife.

When it came time to take the photographs, Jennifer suddenly realized that she had failed to think through this part of her wedding day. She, of course, had envisioned a photograph of herself in her fabulous wedding dress. Jennifer would be standing next to her handsome groom with her father in one picture and her mother in another. But what about Judy?

Her father was obviously trying to push his wife into one of the photographs, and Jennifer could see that her mother was becoming distraught. Jennifer thought if she had to stand between her father and her stepmother, she would surely faint.

The photographer, a seasoned veteran, sensed her distress, and gently pulled her aside. "I know that you would prefer that your stepmother not be in any of your wedding photographs, but your father is helping to pay for your wedding, and would really like a photograph of his wife with you and the groom. Why don't you take a deep breath, smile that beautiful smile of yours, and let me snap a few photos of you and the groom and your father and stepmother. And just remember, when you get your proofs, you don't have to buy the ones with your stepmother in them. Your father, however, probably would love one."

Jennifer, with a little guidance, did as she was told. She noticed later, when going through the proofs, that in the photograph with her father and stepmother, her father was beaming.

It had been a difficult moment for Jennifer, but the photographer had been right to insist on this particular photograph. Jennifer was grateful someone had been there to counsel her.

Photography

Long after everything is said and done, the wedding photographs will be around to remind the bride and groom of the feelings, expressions, tender moments, and special people involved in this important day. The photographs will, if properly planned and professionally taken and developed, give years of pleasure. Careful consideration must be given to both the planning of the photographs—candid and posed—and the selection of the photographer who will take them.

If either the bride's or the groom's parents are divorced, photographic decisions must be thoroughly thought through before the wedding day to avoid awkward situations. Professional photographers have experience with such matters, and can offer expert advice on how to handle certain situations. Choose this person carefully, taking into consideration not only expertise, but tact and sensitivity as well.

Have at least one consultation meeting with the photographer before the wedding. This is crucial when there is a divorce involved. The photographer should be made fully aware of any special circumstances and potential problems within the families.

Divorced parents generally should not appear in the same photograph. If neither parent has remarried and they are friendly, the bride may choose to have them in the photographs together, separated by the bride and groom. Each parent should also have a picture taken with the couple separately.

Whether or not to include stepparents and stepfamilies in the wedding photographs is one of the more difficult decisions the bride and groom will have to make. Having them in the photographs can make for some tense moments if the situation has not been discussed with the photographer ahead of time. Stepparents should be included if they are on friendly terms with the bride and groom. If there is a controversial stepparent, an easy solution is to go ahead and take the picture with the stepparent, remembering that you don't have to buy that one from your proofs. Also, keep in mind that feelings and relationships change through the years, and perhaps, in time, a photograph of your stepparent on this special occasion may become important.

Photography Expenses

The photographic coverage is usually paid for by the bride's family. If the bride's parents are divorced, a decision must be made in advance as to who will pay this expense. It is a nice gesture for the bride's parents to present a few pictures to the groom's parents. His family can then order more from the proofs, and pay for the extras themselves.

Photographers have different ways of charging for their services. Some have flat rates which include a certain number of photographs. Others charge for their time and equipment, as well as for the photographs. After selecting your photographer, a decision should be made as to who will pay his or her fees.

Usually a reputable photographer will require a signed contract and a deposit. This is when the decision must be made as to who will be financially responsible for the photographs. Even if the photographer has a standard contract, be sure to add to it any specific details as to how the expenses will be shared. If they are to be equally shared, both parents need to sign the contract. The parent who signs the contract will ultimately be responsible for the expenses.

Selecting a Photographer

The best way to find a good photographer is to talk with other couples who have been happy with their wedding photographs. Once the choices have been narrowed down, interview the photographer at his studio, where examples of his work can be seen. When talking with him be sure to ask:

• How many pictures will be taken?

• What is the cost of each print? Each album? Is there an additional fee for travel? Does he or she charge for other extras? Most photographers offer wedding "packages" that include a specific number of pictures for a set fee that includes prints and the album. Ask if packages are also available for the parents.

• Find out if the photographer keeps the negatives, and for how long. Consider purchasing them to keep in a safe place, in the event the album is ever lost or damaged.

• Check to see that the photographer's pictures are clear and have good color. Does he or she seem to capture the emotions of the day? Are the photographs creative? Detailed? Flattering? Does the photographer use multiple exposures and split framing, if those are of interest?

During this interview, the bride should get a "feel" for how well the photographer will interact with her family. Remember, the photographer's job will not only be to take wonderful pictures but to treat her special situation with sensitivity.

When to Take Pictures

The photographer needs to arrive at least an hour before the ceremony so that the prewedding photographs listed in this chapter can be taken. The bride may want to take some of her formal posed pictures before the wedding, which saves time after the ceremony and helps the wedding party get to the reception without too much delay. If the bride does not want the groom to see her before the ceremony, take as many pictures as possible without the groom before the wedding, and take the rest after the ceremony.

Videotaping

Videotaping is becoming increasingly popular. Many couples today use videotaping in conjunction with their wedding still photographs. The photographer and the cameraperson, in most cases, work independently and should be introduced to each other prior to the ceremony so they can coordinate their work.

Cameras are lightweight, easy to handle, and easy to operate. The color and quality of the finished tapes have been greatly improved. The most sophisticated videos are shot with two or more cameras. The tapes are edited together, with music and dialogue dubbed in to produce a movielike version of the wedding day. Be sure to consider the following:

- Does the church or synagogue allow videotaping?

- Is there enough light, or will auxiliary lighting be needed?

- Preview other videos the camerperson has done to see if they are the quality and style desired.

- Decide if sound is to be taped during the event, or if it will be dubbed in later.

- Determine the length of the final video wanted.

- Contract for the final product—content and length—in writing, with a total price, and decide who will pay this expense.

Suggested Photographs

The bride should go over the following list of photographs carefully with the groom, her parents, his parents, and the photographer. Everyone should be aware of the photographs to be taken and the time schedule. Be sure to inform all of the wedding party and family members of the exact time for their pictures.

Select the pictures below that apply to your particular situation.

PHOTOGRAPH CHECKLIST

Before the Ceremony

_____ Groom alone

_____ Groom with best man

_____ Groom with groomsmen

_____ Groom with his parents

_____ Groom with his father and/or father and stepmother

_____ Groom with his mother and/or mother and stepfather

_____ Groom with ring bearer

_____ Groom with grandparents

_____ Groom with his brothers and sisters

_____ Bride alone

_____ Bride with honor attendant

_____ Bride with bridesmaids

_____ Bride with her parents

_____ Bride with her mother and/or mother and stepfather

_____ Bride with her father and/or father and stepmother

_____ Bride with flowergirl

_____ Bride putting on garter and placing penny in shoe

_____ Bride with grandparents

_____ Bride with her brothers and sisters

At the Ceremony

_____ Guests arriving

_____ Bride and father (or other escort) going into church or synagogue

_____ Groom's grandparents being seated

_____ Bride's grandparents being seated

_____ Groom's parents being seated, or in procession

_____ Groom's mother and stepfather being seated, or in procession

_____ Groom's stepmother and father being seated, or in procession

_____ Bride's stepmother being seated, or in procession

_____ Bride's mother being seated, or in procession

_____ Bride's mother and stepfather being seated, or in procession

_____ Soloist and organist

_____ Processional

_____ Bride and father (or other escort) starting down aisle

_____ The altar and decorations

_____ Giving-away ceremony

_____ Ring ceremony

_____ Kneeling at altar

_____ Lighting the unity candle

_____ The kiss

_____ Bride and groom coming up the aisle

_____ The recessional

_____ Mothers being ushered out

_____ Bride's stepmother being ushered out

_____ Groom's stepmother being ushered out

_____ Grandparents being ushered out

Posed Pictures, Taken before or after the Ceremony

_____ Entire wedding party, including officiant

_____ Bride and groom with officiant

_____ Bride and groom with bride's parents

_____ Bride and groom with bride's mother and/or mother and stepfather

_____ Bride and groom with bride's father and/or father and stepmother

_____ Bride and groom with groom's parents

_____ Bride and groom with groom's mother and/or mother and stepfather

_____ Bride and groom with groom's father and/or father and stepmother

_____ Bride and groom with bride's grandparents

_____ Bride and groom with groom's grandparents

_____ Bride and groom with her immediate family

_____ Bride and groom with his immediate family

_____ Bride and groom with her mother's immediate family

_____ Bride and groom with her father's immediate family

_____ Bride and groom with his mother's immediate family

_____ Bride and groom with his father's immediate family

_____ Bride and groom

_____ Bride alone

_____ Groom alone

_____ Bride and groom leaving church or synagogue

At the Reception

_____ Bride and groom getting out of the car, if reception is not at church or synagogue

_____ Bride and groom entering the reception

_____ The receiving line

_____ Bride and groom greeting guests in receiving line

_____ Guests signing guest book

_____ Bride and groom dancing

_____ Bride and her father dancing

_____ Groom dancing with bride's mother

_____ Groom dancing with his mother

_____ Bride dancing with groom's father

_____ Parents and stepparents dancing

_____ Bridesmaids and ushers dancing

_____ Guests dancing

_____ The cake table

_____ Bride and groom cutting the cake

_____ Couple feeding cake to each other

_____ Bride and groom receiving toasts

_____ Close-up of ring hands

_____ Buffet tables

_____ The bridal party's table

_____ The parents' tables

_____ Guests' tables

_____ Group photos of special friends

_____ The musicians

_____ Bride tossing the bouquet

_____ Groom taking off the bride's garter

_____ Groom tossing the garter

_____ Bride and groom with whoever catches bouquet and garter

_____ Bride and groom in their going-away clothes

_____ Couple saying goodbye to parents and stepparents

_____ Guests throwing birdseed or flower petals

_____ Decorated getaway car

_____ Bride and groom getting into car

_____ Guests waving goodbye

_____ Couple looking out of rear window as car drives off

_____ Others

Special Photographs

Names of guests photographer shouldn't miss. (Wedding director or some other person should be assigned to point out these people to photographer.)

_____

_____

_____

_____

_____

_____

9

The Reception

Amanda Simpson breathed a sigh of relief. The wedding she and her daughter, Jennifer, had planned for more than a year was as perfect as they'd hoped it would be. As a divorcée who was now happily remarried, Amanda had tried to think of every detail so that everyone—particularly Jennifer—would feel comfortable and happy at the wedding. She was absolutely ecstatic. The rehearsal dinner had been lovely, the ceremony had gone off without a hitch, and now, at the reception, surrounded by family and lifelong friends, it was time to relax and have fun.

The band called for the wedding couple to dance. The guests oohed and aahed over the dress, the setting, the beautiful bride and her handsome husband. This moment, mused Amanda, was worth the headaches, the nightmares, the worrying, the expense. Suddenly, her thoughts were interrupted by an announcement from the band leader: "And now, would the mother and the father of the bride join the wedding couple on the dance floor?"

Immediately, the room grew silent. Everyone turned to find Amanda. Everyone was waiting to see what would happen. Everyone—except the band leader—knew Jennifer's parents were divorced and both were remarried. Amanda pretended she didn't hear the announcement. What else could she do? She and Jennifer's father barely spoke, much less danced.

When planning this wedding, Amanda had tried to predict every problem that could possibly come up, and so far had found solutions for them all. Everything but this. Everything but forgetting to warn the band not to assume that the parents of the bride would take a turn on the dance floor. "It was suddenly all so *real,*" she remembers. "I was the divorced mother of the bride. Even now, it makes my heart pound to think about that moment. My eyes scanned the crowd looking for my new husband. It was apparent that he too was stunned by the band leader's announcement and was making his way to my side. He took my hand and led me to the dance floor, where we joined the bride and groom."

Planning the Reception

The typical bride has spent many hours daydreaming about her reception. She probably knows without question whether she wants a catered dinner in a posh hotel, a buffet and dance out under the stars, or a finger-sandwich tea in the church social hall. But when parents are divorced, that fact alone may help determine the type of reception she chooses. For example, a sit-down dinner or a receiving line with estranged parents may be uncomfortable for everyone.

The bride should think ahead and try to predict how her family will react to the reception she thinks she wants to have. Discuss it with them. Discuss it with the wedding director, or an unbiased outsider. *Then* make the final decision concerning the reception plans. Once this has been done, leave nothing to chance. Map out the reception from start to finish to work out every detail.

Whatever type is chosen, the reception should immediately follow the ceremony. Other considerations when determining the type of reception are the number of guests and the budget.

When parents are divorced, there are certain aspects of the reception that will be handled differently than they would be if there were no divorce in the family. These considerations—such as the receiving line, seating, and dancing—will be discussed in this chapter.

Selecting a Location

Select with care the location for the reception, whether it be a private club, hotel, restaurant, historic home or garden, or in the church or synagogue where the wedding was held. As soon as the choice has been made, check to see if it is available on the wedding day. If it is, reserve it at once. If it is not available, another selection will have to be made, or another date will have to be chosen. Popular locations are sometimes reserved as much as a year in advance.

Ask questions. Find out what is—and is not—included in the cost. Setup? Cleanup? Service fees? Tax? Unexpected costs can add up quickly.

Clubs, Hotels, and Restaurants

Private clubs, hotels, and restaurants are advantageous places for a reception because they offer complete services, and may even have someone on staff who can coordinate the whole event. These places usually require the use of the in-house caterer.

Be sure to:

• Visit the room where the reception will take place. Ask if there will be any changes in the room prior to the reception date (they may be changing the carpeting and completely throw off the decorating scheme). If any renovation is planned, what other arrangements would have to be made?

• Find out what extra fees will be involved in setting up the room for dancing. Will there be an extra charge for a stage and sound system for the band?

• Inquire about a service charge. Ask about staffing, and determine if it will be adequate for the reception.

• Discuss the menu and the cost. Arrange a tasting session if at all possible. Ask if the cost includes a bride's or groom's cake. If not, contract with a bakery.

• Discuss beverage fees separately. Is there a "charge per drink" fee at an open bar? Is there a corking fee if you bring your own wine or champagne? Will nonalcoholic punch be provided? Will coffee be served with the cake?

- Check on any restrictions—music, hours, smoking, number of guests, etc.
- Find out exactly how long the room may be reserved, and plan some way to encourage guests to leave at the appointed time.
- Ask if the in-house florist decorates, or if an outside florist may be used. Compare the quality and cost.

Home or Garden

Having a reception in a private home or garden offers tremendous advantages. The bride can choose the florist and caterer for the exact day and time she wants them. However, there will be no professional staff to take over the details, so it will be up to the bride and/or her family to plan it from setup to cleanup. A friend may be able to help, or, if funds allow, the bride may feel more comfortable hiring a party planner to coordinate the entire event. The wedding director may also help with the reception. In any case, the following checklist may be helpful:

- Make sure the location is large enough to accommodate the guests.
- Check on parking. Is it safe and convenient, or will there be a need to arrange valet service or security?
- Check kitchen and bathroom facilities. Are they adequate?
- Check on the lighting, and the electrical capabilities if there will be a band.
- Decide on how the garden or home will be set up, and determine what equipment will need to be rented.
- Depending on the size and type of reception, the bride may want to prepare much of the food with the help of family and friends. But unless the bride's budget is extremely tight, this is one responsibility she should probably delegate. If the bride chooses

to use a caterer, discuss catering costs. Some caterers charge per person; others will prepare a variety of foods and charge by the dish. Almost all caterers can provide experienced service personnel, including bartenders.

- Send a note to the neighbors letting them know of the reception plans, particularly if there will be a band.

- If planning a garden reception, discuss options in the event of rain. Can the party be moved inside, or could the area be tented?

Churches or Temples

For many brides and grooms, a reception in the social hall in the church or synagogue where the wedding is taking place is the most logical, practical, and desirable location.

Make sure to:

- Find out what is included in the rental fee—setup, cleanup?

- Find out what accessories are provided in the rental fee: chairs, tables, linens, silver?

- Find out if you can bring in your own food and use the kitchen facilities. This is especially important if you are planning a kosher reception. If the church or temple requires a staff member to be present during social functions, ask how much this person will charge.

- Check on musical restrictions.

- Check on alcoholic beverage restrictions.

Types of Receptions

There are several factors that will help the bride determine the type of reception she will have: how well the divorced parents get along, the time of the wedding, the style of the wedding, the size of the wedding, her wishes and desires, and her budget.

Some guidelines based on the hour of the wedding follow.

Morning Receptions

When the bride decides on a morning wedding, a breakfast or brunch is the natural function to follow. She may serve buffet style, or she may have a seated affair.

The menu for a buffet-style breakfast or brunch can be imaginative and relatively inexpensive: fresh fruit, croissants, biscuits or muffins, and several egg-filled casseroles or miniature quiches. Coffee, tea, and orange and tomato juice are perfect accompaniments.

With a sit-down breakfast or brunch, start with the juices and fruit, then serve omelettes, blintzes, or casseroles with toast, biscuits, or muffins. Hot coffee and hot tea are essential.

Pastries and wedding cake can be served after the meal.

If alcoholic beverages are served, there are some wonderful "morning" drinks to choose from: champagne, champagne and orange juice (mimosas), champagne and puréed fresh peaches (peach fuzzies), white wine, screwdrivers, or spicy Bloody Marys.

Luncheon Receptions

These usually follow a late-morning or high-noon wedding and, again, can be buffet style or seated affairs.

The buffet menu can be exciting, but relatively light. It can be primarily salads—shrimp, chicken, pasta, Caesar salad, and fresh fruit. Sandwiches and cheese trays are also filling and popular.

Sit-down luncheons may begin with champagne or cocktails and light hors d'oeuvres. When guests are seated, proceed with a cold or hot soup and wine, then a main course—suitable for lunch.

Coffee and tea are served with the wedding cake as dessert.

Afternoon Receptions

These are usually held between 2:00 P.M. and 5:00 P.M. An afternoon reception can be, and often is, quite simple. Punch, small sandwiches, nuts, and wedding cake are all that is necessary. If the bride chooses to serve alcohol, a nonalcoholic punch and one with champagne may be served. Wine may also be served.

Usually, guests eat standing, or with plates on their laps. It is not necessary to have a table for the bride and her wedding party.

Cocktail Receptions

These are usually held between 4:00 P.M. and 7:30 P.M. Cocktail receptions should begin no later than 6:00 P.M. if dinner or heavy hors d'oeuvres will not be served.

Because the reception is being held during typical "cocktail" hours, the bride may have champagne, wine and beer, or an open bar, depending on her budget.

Always, of course, provide nonalcoholic options, such as punch or soft drinks. The guests may be hungry at this hour, so take that into consideration when planning food quantities. There may be a buffet of hot and cold items, or there may be trays of food passed among the guests.

Dinner Receptions

Dinner receptions usually start between 6:00 P.M. and 9:00 P.M. Cocktails—champagne, wine and beer, or a full bar—and hors d'oeuvres begin the evening, followed by a seated or buffet-style dinner. This type of reception can be costly, but it can also be a lovely way to end the wedding day.

The menu at such a reception is limited only by the tastes and budget of the bride and groom. When selecting the menu, meet with the caterer or the chef at the reception location to discuss various choices. Most formal, seated dinner receptions have a place card for each guest. For less formal seated dinners, place cards are necessary only at the bride's table and the parents' tables.

Dessert can be as simple as a slice of wedding cake or as fancy as baked Alaska. Wine may be served with the dinner and champagne with dessert for toasting.

Reception Schedule of Events

There is no right or wrong schedule for a reception. However, there are some events that traditionally take place at certain times— the bride and groom greet the guests, they cut the wedding cake and share a piece, the bride throws a bouquet and the groom tosses the bride's garter, and the bride and groom depart amid cheers and tears.

The reception should be fun, a time for winding down for the bride and groom and their families after the prewedding whirl-wind. It is a time for the new couple to visit with old and new friends, to say thank you, to introduce each other. The reception should, by all means, be flexible enough to allow for a few minutes' leeway here and there.

A few things the bride may want to keep in mind when planning:

• If at all possible, try to avoid a long line forming for the guests to sign the guest book (or bride's book) or to speak to the people in the receiving line, if there is one. If the line becomes too long, the director or someone else should help move people along. They may suggest that guests go directly into the room where refreshments are being served, and encourage them to come back when the receiving line isn't so long.

• When the guests first arrive, it is polite to serve them something to drink while they mingle and wait to speak to the bride and groom. Drinks may be passed, or the guests may go directly into the reception area to get their own drinks.

• A wedding director or competent friend should be asked to help make the reception run smoothly. This person is essential, in addition to the caterer, who should be in charge of the kitchen.

Two suggested reception schedules follow.

Dinner Reception Schedule

First Half Hour

Receiving line is formed, if there is one.

Drinks are served as guests visit.

Music begins.

After One Hour

Dinner or buffet is announced and guests are seated, if there is going to be a seated party.

A blessing may be given by the officiant or a family friend.

Best man gives a toast to the bride and groom. Groom may offer a toast to his best man, to the bride, to her parents and/or his parents.

Other toasts are given.

The music resumes.

After One and a Half Hours

First course is cleared from the table.

Dance music begins.

First dance by bride and groom.

Other traditional dances (remember to warn the band if there are unusual circumstances as the result of a divorce, so that they do not inadvertently ask divorced couples to dance).

Guests begin to dance.

After Two Hours

Tables are cleared.

Cake is cut and bride and groom share the first slice.

Cake is served to guests, with parents being served first.

Dancing resumes.

Last Half Hour

Bride throws her bouquet, or a smaller bouquet made for this purpose, to her single women guests.

Groom takes the bride's garter, after he removes it from her leg, and throws it to the bachelors.

Bride and groom may change before going away, but many choose to leave in their wedding attire if they are staying in town that night.

Guests gather to toss birdseed or flower petals to the bride and groom as they leave.

Parents discreetly tell band to stop playing and bar to close when they are ready to leave.

Reception Schedule for Other than Seated Dinner

Receiving line is formed, if there is one.

Drinks are served as guests arrive.

Background music is playing.

Dancing begins with bride and groom's traditional first dance. (This is sometimes done as soon as the bride and groom arrive at the reception.)

Cake is cut and bride and groom share the first slice.

Dancing resumes.

Bride throws her bouquet, or a smaller bouquet made for this purpose, to her single women guests.

Groom takes the bride's garter, after he removes it from her leg, and throws it to the bachelors.

Bride and groom may change before going away, but many choose to leave in their wedding attire if they are staying in town that night.

Guests gather to toss birdseed or flower petals to the bride and groom as they leave.

Parents discreetly tell band to stop playing and bar to close when they are ready to leave.

The Receiving Line

The reception may begin with a receiving line, a nice way to greet guests and thank them for being with your family on such a special day. If the wedding is small, the family may wish to greet guests informally outside the church immediately after the ceremony, instead of waiting until the reception. If the bride chooses to have a receiving line, she must decide where it will be placed. Choose a spot that allows for easy traffic flow, and where there will be ample room to set up a table for the bride's book or guest book. The book could be set up before the receiving line, so that guests can sign it as they wait, or located so that guests will sign it just after going through the line.

The bride should plan ahead of time who will stand in the receiving line. When parents are divorced, this can sometimes be awkward. Many brides and grooms today are choosing to eliminate the formal receiving line entirely. Some simply choose to stand alone without their families. If, however, the bride wants her parents to stand in the receiving line, divorced parents should not stand together, unless they are very friendly and are hosting the reception together. If the bride's mother and stepfather are hosting the wedding, the mother alone or she and her husband are in line, but the father is not. If the bride's father and stepmother are giving the wedding, they are the host and hostess, and therefore stand in the receiving line. The bride's mother is an honored guest and does not stand in the line. If the bride's parents are divorced and neither is remarried, only the bride's mother would stand in the receiving line, unless the father is giving the reception. In that case, the father could ask his mother, the bride's aunt, or the bride's godmother to stand in line and act as hostess with him. When the groom's parents are divorced, only the mother stands in line with her son, eliminating the necessity of asking, or excluding, his father or stepfather.

Here are some suggested arrangements for a receiving line when parents are divorced. They begin with the first person guests will greet in the line.

Receiving Line Arrangements

Most Traditional
Bride's mother
Groom's mother
Bride and groom
Maid or matron of honor and bridesmaids (optional)

Bride's Mother and Stepfather Hosting Reception
Bride's mother and stepfather. (Father is a guest and not in the
  receiving line.)
Groom's parents
Bride and groom
Maid or matron of honor and bridesmaids (optional)

Bride's Father and Stepmother Hosting Reception
Bride's father and stepmother. (Mother is a guest and not in the
  receiving line.)
Groom's parents
Bride and groom
Maid or matron of honor and bridesmaids (optional)

Bride's Father Hosting Reception Alone
Bride's father. (He may ask his mother, the bride's aunt, or the
  bride's godmother to stand with him.)
Groom's parents
Bride and groom
Maid or matron of honor and bridesmaids (optional)

Reception Hosted by Persons Other than Bride's Parents
Host and hostess
Groom's parents
Bride and groom
Maid or matron of honor and bridesmaids (optional)

Bride's Mother, Father, and Stepmother Hosting Reception
Bride's mother
Groom's parents
Bride and groom
Bride's stepmother and father. (Unless the stepmother is very close
   to the bride, she may choose not to stand in the receiving line.)
Maid or matron of honor and bridesmaids (optional)

At very large, formal weddings, the bride may choose to have an
announcer, who stands next to each guest as he or she approaches
the receiving line and quietly asks for his or her name, which is then
repeated aloud. This can be helpful when there are a great number
of guests whom the bride's mother does not know.

The guests move down the line, shaking hands with the mothers
of the wedding couple, and shaking hands or kissing the new-
lyweds, depending on how well they know them.

The first person in the receiving line, whether it is the bride's
mother, stepmother, or father, is responsible for introducing guests
to the groom's mother, and to the bride if necessary. The bride
then turns to the groom and introduces him to the guest. The
groom, naturally, introduces his bride to his friends.

If the receiving line becomes too long, the director or someone
else should help move people along. He or she may suggest that
guests go directly into the room where refreshments are being
served and encourage them to come back when the receiving line is
shorter.

Seating Arrangement

If the bride's parents are divorced, a formal seating arrangement at
the reception should not be a great problem since the bride and
groom are seated with only their wedding party at the "bride's
table." Parents and stepparents are seated at their own tables, called
the "parents' tables." At most receptions, these are the only tables
with place cards reserving specific places for honored guests.

Divorced parents are not seated together at the parents' table. If
they are friendly, the parent who is giving the reception could

invite the other parent, but will seat him or her at another table. Stepparents are included at the table.

If the divorce has been bitter, it might be better for the parent who is not giving the wedding reception to attend only the marriage ceremony and not the reception. If the bride and groom insist, however, the father or mother may come for a short time, but his or her spouse should tactfully stay away.

Following are suggested seating charts for the reception.

Seating arrangement with head table

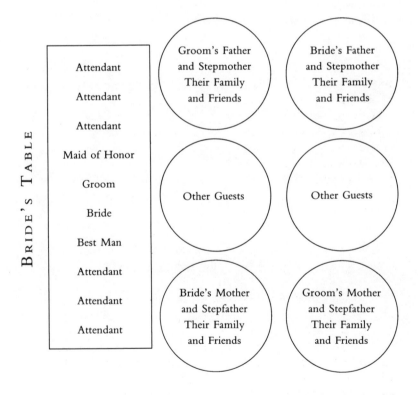

Place cards are not necessary at a reception except at the bride's table and the parents' tables.

Seating arrangement without head table

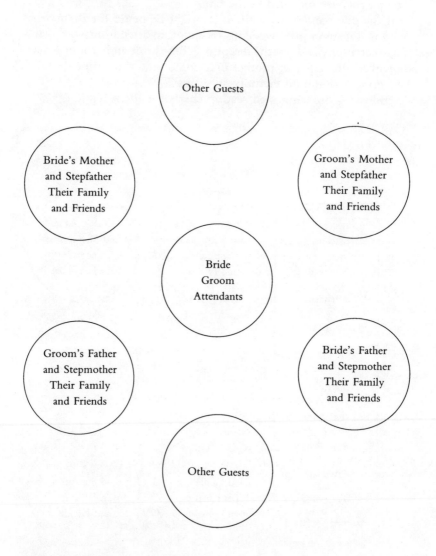

Place cards are not necessary at a reception except at the bride's table and the parents' tables.

Dancing

Dancing is not necessary, particularly if the bride and groom want a simple reception, but it does add a festive touch and many of the guests will enjoy it. Music may be provided by an orchestra, a band, a string trio, a piano, a disc jockey, or even a stereo.

When the bride's or groom's parents are divorced, the formal, traditional order of dancing can be eliminated. The only tradition that should be observed is for the bride and groom to have the first dance, signaling to the guests that they, too, may join in. Remind the wedding director, or whoever is in charge, to tell the band leader or master of ceremonies not to request that the parents of the wedding couple dance together—possibly an embarrassing situation when they are divorced.

If the bride chooses to have formal dancing, the bride and groom begin by dancing to a favorite song. Then the bride's father may break in, and the groom may ask his new mother-in-law to dance. If the bride's parents are divorced and she does not want to choose between her father and her stepfather, she may invite everyone to dance after she has danced with the groom for a short while. Alternatively, if the bride's father escorted her down the aisle at the wedding, perhaps her stepfather, who raised her or to whom she is close, can be the first to break in on the bride and groom. As with all other aspects of planning a wedding with divorced parents, this will vary according to the circumstances. But by no means leave it to chance!

At a large reception, the bride may want guests to begin dancing right after they've been through the receiving line. Her father or the host can encourage them to do so. Then, after she has greeted her guests, the band can signal to the guests to clear the floor with a drumroll, and the bride and groom can have the traditional first dance.

If the reception is a sit-down dinner, the first course is served soon after the bridal party is seated. Dancing may begin after the first course is cleared from the table. However, if the reception follows a late-afternoon wedding, and the meal will not be served until later, dancing can begin before the wedding party is seated. At a buffet reception, the bride and groom may start the dancing as soon as they have greeted their guests.

The father of the groom and the best man usually dance with the bride after her father and/or stepfather, and the groom dances with his mother-in-law and then his mother or stepmother. The groom will then dance with the maid or matron of honor, the ushers will dance with the bridesmaids, and then guests can begin to join in.

Conclusion

≈

This book took two and a half years to research and write. Even when rereading the manuscript for the final time, we realized that there were situations that had occurred with clients and friends that we had not mentioned. We have tried to cover the most common situations and hope you will be able to use our examples as a starting point for planning your own wedding.

Our final thoughts on planning a wedding with divorced parents are: Be flexible. Be considerate. If possible, enlist the help of an impartial person, preferably a professional wedding consultant. And above all, remember: The wedding is the bride and groom's special day.

Acknowledgments

We would like to thank the following people for their generous support and friendship: Bruce Feiler for his guidance, Martha Newbit for her expertise, and Cathy Joyner and Cheryl Terry for their countless hours at the computer.

A special thanks to these friends for their encouragement along the way: Joy, Susan, Jane, Lois, Polly, Gerald, and Tom, who renamed our book "Where to Sit When You're Split."

A very special thank you to our agent, Jane Dystel, who immediately recognized the need for our book, and to our editor, Erica Marcus, who led us through the book step by step.

Finally, we would like to express our warmest appreciation and love to the members of our families, especially to Tracy, whose wedding was our inspiration, and to the other brides and grooms, particularly those with divorced parents, whose experiences helped shape this book.

Index

190

Notes

Notes